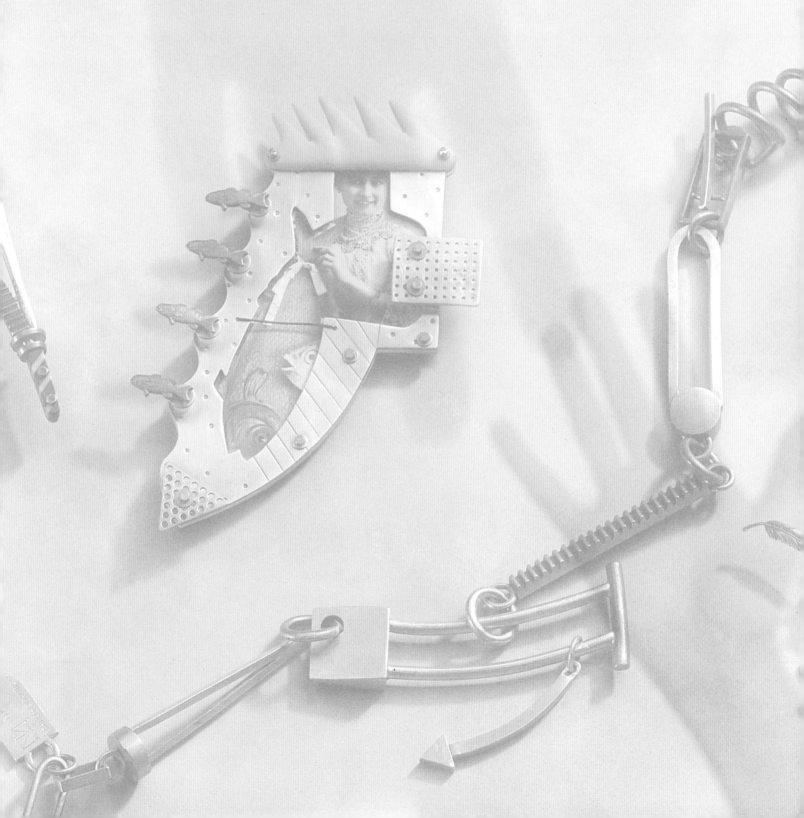

thomas mann
METAL ARTIST

ANDREI CODRESCU

LLOYD E. HERMAN

Foreword by Michael W. Monroe

GUILD Publishing • Madison, Wisconsin

Distributed by North Light Books, Cincinnati, Ohio

THOMAS MANN

Metal Artist

Andrei Codrescu • Lloyd E. Herman

Published by GUILD Publishing
931 E. Main Street, Madison, Wisconsin 53703
TEL 608-257-2590 • FAX 608-257-2690
www.guild.com

Chief editorial officer: Katie Kazan
Cover and interior design: Cheryl Smallwood-Roberts

Distributed by North Light Books
An imprint of F&W Publications, Inc.
1507 Dana Avenue, Cincinnati, OH 45207
TEL 800-289-0963

ISBN: 1-893164-12-8
Printed in China

JACKET: *Mermaid*, 1991, from the *Collage Box & Brooch* series, wood, glass, acrylic, silver, gold leaf, nickel, brass,
antique photograph. Removable, wearable brooch: 2" x 6"; box: 8" x 5" x 14"; backboard box: 23" x 3" x 26".
One of twelve pieces made for a touring exhibition. Collection of Elsie Michie. Photography by Will Crocker.

ENDPAPERS (left to right): *Outline Heart Pin*, 1992, silver, bronze, copper, 1.75" x 2.5". *Eye of the Beholder:
Space Frame Neckpiece,* 1992, silver, bronze, brass, acrylic, black onyx, fiberglass, laminated acrylic, 1.5" x 5.5".
A Girl and Her Fish, 1990, photo collage pin, silver, nickel, stainless steel, bronze, micarta, aluminum, antique
photograph, brass, 2" x 3.5". *Big Link Fetish Necklace*, 1992, silver, brass, bronze, copper, 32" long. *Eye Pin*, 1991,
bronze, silver, brass, 3" x 3". *Oriole*, 1990, collage bird pin from *Aviatrix* series, silver, bronze, acrylic, paper, 3" x
2.5". Hands pictured are those of coworkers Helma Mezey, Jane Decuers, Mark Garcie, Ralph Cole and Courtney
Miller. Art direction by Aimee Farnet. Photography by Will Crocker.

FRONTISPIECE: *Homage à Oskar Schlemmer*, 2000, from the traveling exhibition "Attitude & Action," curated
by Gail M. Brown, *Collage Box Neckpiece*, nickel, silver, bronze, micarta, acrylic, glow-in-the-dark acrylic, 4" x
5.5" x .6". Collection of the artist.

THIS PAGE: *Self-Portrait (just me)*, 1995, from the *Self-Portrait Brooch* series, brass, bronze, micarta, photo, laminated acrylic, 2.75" x 4.5".

PAGE 6: *Ltd. Edition Teapot Necklace*, 1997, silver, brass, bronze, nickel, micarta, laminated acrylic, centerpiece:
3" x 2.5". The tea container in this piece removes to become a functional tea infuser.

PAGE 7: *X32*, from *La Cabeza Brooch* series, 1998, silver, bronze, glow-in-the-dark acrylic, laminated acrylic,
3.25" x 4". Photo: Gerrod Perrone

CONTENTS

FOREWORD

Michael W. Monroe

THOMAS MANN IS A VISUAL MAGICIAN AND A POET. HIS JEWELRY AND SCULPTURAL objects convey a delightful voyage through an intriguing world of possibilities. Entering a display of his works is equal to turning backflips into the playground of one's youth.

Perpetually challenging our habitual modes of perception, Mann is fascinated with the flotsam and jetsam of our lives. Entirely or in part, the constituent elements of his art are either manufactured parts or natural objects and fragments not intended as art materials. Intrinsic to "assemblage" (an art form originating in the 20th century and integral to surrealism, dadaism, constructivism and American abstract expressionism) is the evocative, witty and baffling inclusion of objects — simple, real and honest — into compositions. Mann extends this rich tradition into the 21st century. His goal is to strike sparks from unrelated, incongruous, contradictory materials and ideas, and thereby lift us out of our humdrum lives; in doing so, he transmutes physical materials and their auras into new amalgams. He poses significant and sophisticated contrasts between folk and fine art, and between pictorial and genuine reality. Mann sees the use of real objects as vehicles for the free exercise of his poetic imagination and what at first appear to be unexpected and incongruous juxtapositions are, in fact, based upon thematic and formal considerations. He incorporates reality into his jewelry without imitating reality. He prefers to work with the raw materials of life, rather than art.

Thomas Mann's quick and direct methods of creating mesh perfectly with our quickened sense of time. He metamorphoses cast-off fragments of daily life into spiritual entities that, because of their associations, reach to the origins of human consciousness and the depth of human possibility.

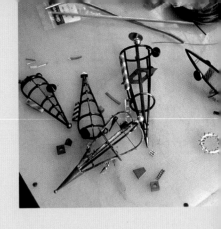

THOMAS MANN
AN APPRECIATION

Lloyd E. Herman

THOMAS MANN HAS BEEN IN THE VANGUARD OF AMERICAN ART JEWELRY DESIGN FOR nearly three decades. His compositions were among the first to focus not on the intrinsic value of precious metals and gemstones, but rather on idea and content. Following the collage/assemblage strategies of early-20th-century sculptors, he combines silver and non-precious metal elements with plastics and found elements. His distinctive wearable pieces — "jewelry objects," as he likes to call them — and his sculpture have been included in national and international traveling art exhibitions; collected by art museums; sold in shops, galleries and museum stores; written about; and worn by proud collectors.

Recognizing beauty and novelty in small objects that were made for other uses, and incorporating them into jewelry, is nothing new. Tribal cultures worldwide have been fascinated by items unusual to them, such as safety pins, tokens and coins, and have used them in handmade objects for body adornment. Picasso's famous sculpture of a bull's head, composed of a bicycle handlebar and seat, is arguably the world's most famous example of found-object sculpture. The found-object tradition persists today in the art of many university-educated jewelers, as well as self-taught artists once considered "naive." We now recognize sophistication in so-called outsider art, and admire it in museums alongside objects of great refinement — some of which are also made from nontraditional materials.

ABOVE: View of light box next to workbench, with *Space Neckpieces* in progress.

OPPOSITE: *Mythos Vanity*, 1994, installation view, Gallery I/O, wood, glass paint, steel wire, galvanized steel, stones, found objects, 28" x 21" x 29".

Though Mann has created thousands of unique objects in his career, nearly every one is immediately identifiable as originating in his fertile imagination. Other jewelry artists in America and elsewhere have discovered the tactile and visual pleasures of plastics, base metals and found objects, but no one else has sustained — and expanded on — a distinctive style as has Thomas Mann. The range and quantity of his creative output are astonishing.

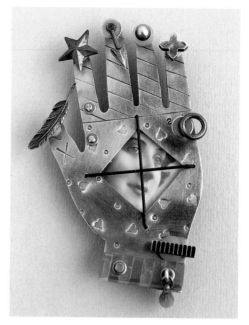

Collage Photo Hand Pin, 1990, silver, brass, bronze, photo, laminated acrylic, found objects, 1.75" x 2.5". Collection of Elissa Topol and Lee Osterman.

INFLUENCES

Thomas Mann is certainly a sophisticate in his use of the found object. His sure sense of composition, his ability to recognize an intriguing shape in a familiar (or unfamiliar) cast-off or industrial part, is more akin to Picasso than to Simon Rodia, whose folk art masterwork, the Watts Towers in Los Angeles, incorporates a multitude of found elements such as bottle caps, seashells, and fragments of glass and china.

"Back in the late sixties, while I was majoring in theater," the artist says, "I was heavily influenced by the collage and assemblage techniques of Joseph Cornell, Man Ray, Marcel Duchamp, and especially by Picasso and Georges Braque. Their thinking about art and their art-making was totally new and peculiar to the 20th century. Later, after college, I took on the personal challenge to find my own way to apply these influences and techniques in the making of jewelry objects.

"Potent models were presented to me in the work of contemporary American and European metal artists and teachers, and they confirmed my desire to move in this direction. J. Fred Woell and Bob Ebendorf proved that you could have a lot of fun making found-object work. Anton Cepka, Claus Bury and Herman Junger combined alternative, nonprecious materials with precious metals and gems. And all of them exhibited the influences of the 20th century's most dramatic art movements: the cubists, surrealists, dadaists, Italian futurists, Russian constructivists, and abstract modernists. I felt like a kid in the art candy store, absorbing and chewing and hoping to spit out my own version of all of these influences."

Around 1945, at the experimental Black Mountain College in North Carolina, innovative jewelry was made by artists Anni Albers and Alex Reed. Like Marcel Duchamp, they found beauty in "readymades" and fashioned necklaces from such disparate elements as spark plugs, sink drain plates, and paper clips. Thomas Mann's similar use of industrial products available in any hardware store thus links him to mid-20th-century art-making philosophies, as well as those from early in the century.

PARTS AND NAMES FOR A DISTINCTIVE STYLE

Though Mann initially incorporated true found objects in his jewelry, he found that for multiples production he needed parts that were more readily and reliably available. His sources included electronic instrument parts from surplus stores servicing the Kennedy Space Center in Florida, costume jewelry parts, lighting supply houses, inventor supply resources, musical instrument machine shops, and model train manufacturers. His staff manipulates all of these parts and pieces, and fabricates them into proprietary elements.

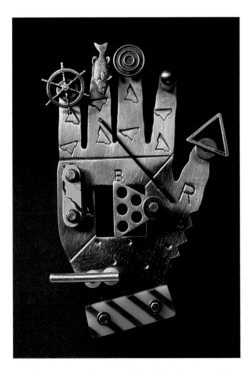

Hand Pin, 1996, laminated acrylics, bronze, silver, 1.75" x 2.5".

In-house, plastic parts have always been sawn by hand, but more and more often, Mann sends this kind of work to laser-cutting services that were originally developed to support the space industry. Chemical machining, better known as "photo etching," is used to extract his design components from metal sheet. This laborsaving technique produces parts identical to those that are hand sawn.

"I love to use materials that smack of high-tech: perforated metals, laminated acrylics, electronic components, coaxial cables and the like," Mann says. Though there is no gold or other highly polished metal in Mann's jewelry, there is a richness imparted by the natural tones of stainless steel, silver, nickel, aluminum, brass, bronze and copper. Plastics such as acrylic, nylon, fiberglass and micarta (a cellulose-based plastic from the 1940s, and a favorite of the artist) provide contrast.

"In 1977, I made a conscious decision to pursue the course I'd been experimenting with for the previous four years. This decision changed everything. I made the decision not to follow the precious-metals path as a jewelry designer, but to follow, instead, the course of the artist working in the medium of jewelry. This is an important distinction because I don't consider myself a jeweler. I didn't want to make jewelry that was valued for its precious-material content, but rather for its message or story. With this path, the material choices were much more varied and interesting, and the opportunity for expression much broader. And I wanted to keep the price down so more people could afford the work.

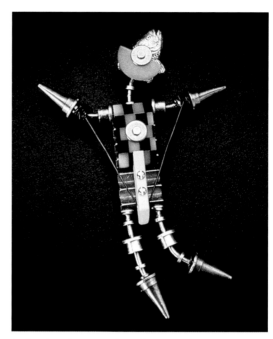

Redi-Kilo Fish, 1982, silver, aluminum, brass, acrylic, laminated acrylic, 2" x 3".

"But this decision has changed everything, right down to the present, because it forced me to do things I had avoided by choosing to be an artist. Because eventually, in order to achieve the rewards that my artistic efforts had produced, I had to become much more of a businessman than I'd ever imagined.

"I've used a succession of terms to define my work. At first, in the late seventies, I called my pieces 'Heartwear,' which suggested post-hippie mysticism, and was also a pun on 'hardware.' In the early eighties, as I was incorporating primitive multicultural design influences, I called the work 'Future Primitive Jewelry Objects.' But I received a cease-and-desist letter from some folks on the West Coast who happened to own the trademark on that name, so I quickly moved on to 'Para-Normal Jewelry Objects,' and sometimes 'New Wave Techno-Freneticism.' Then, shortly after this, I came up with the term 'Techno-Romantic,' which seemed to encompass all of the previous terms, and which I immediately trademarked!"

Though Mann's style was influenced by exemplars from the sculpture and metal-smithing fields, his production methods had different models. The process of designing and producing multiples — of jewelry and domestic objects such as mirror frames, clocks and furniture — probably has more in common with the ateliers of designer

Philippe Starck or glass superstar Dale Chihuly. Like them, Mann employs others to realize his design/art concepts.

Reaching farther back into the history of the decorative arts we can also see Mann's antecedents in the studio of Louis Comfort Tiffany (in the United States) or the House of Faberge (in Russia). Both Tiffany and Faberge designed unique luxury goods as well as production designs that included jewelry and elegant, refined tabletop objects. Mann has become widely known for such multiples, but the unique pieces he makes each year permit him to test ideas that might later be refined in production designs.

THE MANN STORY

Unlike most other leading jewelry artists and designers, Thomas Mann is the product of neither a conventional university nor an art school education as a product designer or

Wounded Heart Neckpiece, 1986, silver, bronze, aluminum, brass, acrylic, laminated acrylic, copper, steel, 4.5" x 5.5".

jeweler-metalsmith. In Allentown, Pennsylvania, where the Mann family lived, the high school Tom attended had a strong art curriculum. One semester of this curriculum focused on jewelry making. When C. Leslie Smith, a student of Richard Rhinehardt at the Philadelphia College of Art, opened a silversmith shop in Allentown, the boy went to work there part time, finishing and polishing Smith's Scandinavian-influenced designs. He also worked at Cinruss Creations, another shop in the city, where he learned fabrication skills. Soon, the sixteen-year-old jewelry maker was taking his own bangle bracelets to sell in the halls at school, bringing home as much as $200 for a week's work.

The jewelry that Thomas Mann made in high school, and later in college, helped to pay his way through East Stroudsburg University. Since the school didn't offer an art major, he started his college career majoring in physical education — but for several semesters he forged his

Exhibition invitation for *Collage/Assemblage,* designed by Thomas Mann.

advisor's signature in order to take every music, art and philosophy course he could get in to. Eventually, he graduated with a degree in Performing Arts.

Mann's signature "Techno-Romantic" style — which had been developing since 1977 — debuted at the Milwaukee Lakefront Art Festival in 1980. It was the first full collection of Mann's jewelry that was not based on the neo-Scandinavian style he had followed since he began making jewelry in high school in 1963. At the Milwaukee festival, "this new look was all I showed," Mann says. "I was dead broke, but I didn't take any polished silver, anything to fall back on. I won a prize and sold everything I brought."

The "techno" aspect includes references to machine parts, electronic components, aircraft design and home appliances. Such items are collaged with images of the human form, references to food, and such familiar shapes as hearts, old photographs and other comforting symbols. These "romantic" elements soften the hard-edged industrial materials used in the work, and hint at a narrative underlying the piece. At various times, Mann has also incorporated polished semiprecious stones and even neon into his work.

Tom Mann began coming to New Orleans from his home in New Hampshire in 1977. Initially, he came to show his work at the New Orleans Jazz & Heritage Festival, but before long he was renting space there for six months in winter and spring, making "jewelry objects" and considering his future. Industrial buildings and commercial real estate suitable for artists' studios was becoming expensive in New England in the 1980s, and the young metalsmith realized that parts of New Orleans held relative bargains for astute real estate shoppers.

Today, Mann is an active member of the art establishment in his adopted hometown. The dozen art and craft fairs across the country where he sells his jewelry include not only the Jazz & Heritage Festival in New Orleans, but also the Arts Council of New Orleans' Fresh Art Festival, which he helped establish. In 1993, Mann created a large steel sculpture in New Orleans' Behrman Park, and his bas relief sculptures for pediments of two streetcar stops along the waterfront of the

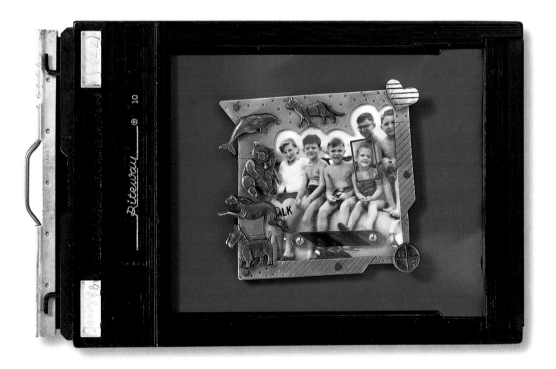

Shirley and the Kids, 1984, photo-collage pin, silver, brass, bronze, laminated acrylic, found objects. Collection of Shirley Drevich.

French Quarter add a dash of Techno-Romantic to the city's historic charm. In 2000, he designed and built the furniture used on the set of "The Real World" television show during the season it originated from New Orleans.

The opportunity to design the furniture for "The Real World" is only one of Mann's links to film and video productions in the Queen City. During the filming of *Dead Man Walking* several years ago, actor-director Tim Robbins purchased Mann's jewelry for Susan Sarandon; later, she came to the gallery herself to buy additional pieces. Mann's jewelry has also been worn on television by Whoopi Goldberg (on the David Letterman show), and shown by Oprah Winfrey on her program. Robin Williams and Cher both own Mann jewelry.

Baby Heart, 1982, photo-collage pin, acrylic, silver, brass, photo, silver, antique photograph, 1.25" x 2".

HEARTS, BIG AND SMALL

Like the repeated hand motif, hearts are quickly recognized as a sign of a Thomas Mann design. His current public art project is a twenty-two-foot-tall "caged" heart for the Paige Campbell Heart Institute at Vanderbilt University in Nashville; it's Mann's first public art commission outside New Orleans. The skeletal aluminum sculpture will sit atop a ten-foot pedestal at the corner of a new entry wing.

The recurring heart icon represents the "romantic" aspect of his Techno-Romantic style. Hearts appear in both flat and fully three-dimensional form in his jewelry and in skeleton form represented in the sculpture for Vanderbilt. The industrial materials of the "techno" aspect lend themselves readily to enlarging the jewelry scale of Mann's designs to full sculptural size.

Moon Bow, 1992, photo-collage pin, acrylic, nickel, photo, silver, aluminum, antique photograph, 1.5" x 3".

Heart Pond, 2000, brooch from the *Float* series, silver, aluminum, micarta, laminated acrylic, 3" x 4".

Porthole, 1991, photo-collage pin, acrylic, bronze, antique photo, silver, aluminum, 2" x 3" x .25".

THOMAS MANN, BUSINESSMAN

Along with the sculpture studio and the workspace where other departments make and assemble Mann's production designs, a gallery in the artist's two side-by-side buildings sells the work of both Mann and other artists. The gallery brings in about one-quarter of the company's income; other direct sales come through the thomasmann.com website. The work is also available through 250 stores and galleries nationally and internationally.

One-of-a-kind pieces are never profitable, the artist confides, though he may make and sell as many as 350 in any year. But his unique pieces often become prototypes for production, and they help promote the roughly 250 production designs in the Techno-Romantic line each year. That number remains fairly constant. Tom and his staff annually evaluate the line for items that have not sold well and replace them with new production items derived from the unique prototypes. Some items in the production line have been in continuous production since the late 1970s.

From the moment he realized that to be profitable his jewelry must be made in multiples, Tom has constantly refined his business methods. "Artists often underprice their work because they think in terms of their own pocketbooks," he says. "They think, 'Well, how much would I pay for something like this?' and fail to realize that their clients may be willing and able to pay much more. They may not consider all of the components that go into pricing, and the rising cost of everything from materials to shipping. They don't think about next year, when everything will go up." Mann's business acumen is held in high regard in the craft community, and the course he designed in 1989 and introduced at the Penland School of Crafts, "Design for Survival," is now on video.

Television and movies often feed Mann's creative energy, providing the germ of visual ideas that turn up later in jewelry or other objects. He particularly likes the unique visual style of *Blade Runner* and *Waterworld,* but he has other favorite movies that he may watch dozens of time for pure enjoyment. Besides watching movies — and his favorite cooking shows on television — what does this supercharged artist and businessman do in his spare time?

"Sometimes," he says, "when I'm working at night, which often is the case, I'll stop whatever one-of-a-kind piece I am working on and just start on something for a friend or family member or just for myself. Then it's hobby time. My hobby is making things and my job, my career, is making things! Sometimes I'll put a model airplane together or an electronic kit. To me, building a model plane is the same as making jewelry or designing a sculpture. Cooking is the same as making jewelry, especially sushi. Working on my sailboat is like making jewelry. I love what I do. I love making things. It's what I'm here for."

ABOVE: Original sketch for the *Caged Heart Sculpture* series, drawn on a restaurant tablecloth, 1997.
OPPOSITE: 1995

THOMAS MANN
THE NONPRECIOUS PATH

Andrei Codrescu

Tom's office, one floor above his production studio, looks like the inside of a mad clock, not unlike one of his jewels. Sculptural assemblages and seemingly random objects startle me every time I look up from the several hundred slides that Tom has selected ("out of 5,000") to represent his work. Five thousand one-of-a-kind objects! I am quite certain that I have not written that many poems. And even if I had, poems are made only of words, not metals, glass, plastics, stone, wood, paper, bone, and even mysterious fragments of language! Most of these objects are small and intricate, their production requiring eons of patience and an unfailingly steady hand. Some pieces are parts of a series, like long dreams unfolding in installments over many nights; some start small and grow big, others spawn offspring, and all, without exception, sport some incongruity, a clash of elements. There are peppers with clockworks inside; extravagant eyeglasses pushed past the requirements of a human face; frames made from wheels and buttons; photographs meshed with machine parts, *milagros* and circuit boards; boxes enclosing mechanical-aviary creatures; books carved up to hide pseudo-religious fetishes, fragments of license plates and house numbers. This is a world of fusing realms, of natural and artificial colliding objects that have renounced their familiar uses to become Thomas Mann works. Readjust your lenses, ladies and gentlemen, we are spinning down a nonlinear and quite bountiful meditation on past, present and future.

OPPOSITE: *Play Pins,* brooches, 1997, resin, acrylic, found objects, various sizes.

Therefore, it is not surprising that Thomas Mann, the namesake of a great German writer whom he does not resemble in the least, turns out to be some sort of whirling intellectual dervish. When I ask him how he arrives at his ideas for art, he cautiously replies, "I make things. Now and then I make art. I make occasions for art to take place." But when I ask him who has influenced him, he tells me without hesitating, "The dadaists and the surrealists. Marcel Duchamp, Joseph Cornell, Man Ray. Alexander Calder." Then he remembers, "Calder made jewelry. He started small, with precise maquettes."

Solar Wind, Tom's second retail store adventure, Stone Harbor, NJ, 1969. Mural and logo by the artist.

The artists Tom mentions are all, with the possible exception of Calder, men who were against traditional definitions of art and reality. They were also Europeans or, at least, exiles. Ironically, they are now part of the history of art, natives of a new country called Modern Art. The irony does not escape Tom, who thinks of himself as an adopted citizen of that country, naturalized generationally. When he came of age in the mid-to-late sixties, America was at war, half his generation was at war with the war, and life was de facto surreal.

In 1963, in high school, he took a silversmithing course and made bracelet-bangles that he sold out of a sock. He made money. His mother thought that he was selling drugs. As the war became the predominant fact of American life, young people elaborated an entire philosophy of life based on utopian hope. Boys started wearing jewelry. The rebel American body changed its stylistic requirements, reaching through history for shapes that made spiritual sense. Archaic cultures seemed suddenly more relevant and connected to nature than wasteful American consumerism. Between the Vietnam casualty reports on television and the Blakean visions of hippies, American life became an endless

1974

Tom at the workbench, Earthlight Supply in its first incarnation. At this time, the silversmith shop was located in the natural food store, 1972.

Have a Nice Ride, 1980, container pin, bronze, silver, acrylic, NY subway token, 3" x 2.5".

Earthlight Supply, the natural food store owned by Mann and his brother, East Stroudsburg, PA, 1974. Signage and logo by the artist.

performance, part theater of the absurd, part Greek tragedy. Everyday objects took on a religious aura. Every gesture was fraught with meaning, the absurdity of which was quickly evident, so that laughter was the one steady measure. The odd texture of those days was entirely too artistic in its daily unfolding to give birth to much "art."

One of the very few entirely specific expressions of the decade was crafts. I remember well the fetish-power of jewelry in the late 1960s and the culture of jewel-making in the hippie enclaves of San Francisco and beyond. The jeweler was a kind of shaman who fashioned power objects: amulets for protection against a hostile system, and love jujus for personal and communal use. Jewelry was also a kind of bridge between folk and high art, a distinction that the hippies did their best to abolish. The young rebels of America adopted for their uses all the art that seemed to them to serve their utopian, visionary purposes, while providing, at the same time, a critique of the "straight" world. The dadaist and surrealist artists were the ideal models because they had rejected, under similar historical conditions, the whole notion of art as a luxury for the rich. Instead, they saw artistic activity as a means of changing consciousness and society. Such a conceit involved, in addition to the spontaneous (and often accidental) creation of objects, a constant and dramatic engagement with the world. Their preeminent means of making art was collage and assemblage that brought together seemingly incongruous elements in order to create shock and surprise. They also sought to abolish the borders between different art genres: poets collaborated with artists, musicians, filmmakers, set designers, dancers, playwrights. They incorporated archaic arts and explored the magical traditions of "primitive" cultures.

1987

The hippies were the inheritors of this artistic revolution, but they adopted other traditions as well, particularly those of the arts and crafts movement and the flowing shapes of the pre-Raphaelite painters. There is a treatise to be written here on the various artistic currents that America's counterculture made its own in the late sixties and seventies, but what matters is that all the borrowing was only for the purpose of creating an authentic art of its own. That art was most successful in music, comic art and jewelry; very little "high" art or writing survived the decade and a half. When the social revolution wound down and yesterday's rebels put down their funny hats, the only visible symbols remaining were songs (soon to be used in car commercials), comic books (sponged up by MTV) and certain "psychedelic" shapes that were gobbled up by fashion.

On the other hand, the invisible work of the revolution continued unabated because it had become a permanent part of the consciousness of many working artists. Just as the ideas advanced by the dadaists and the surrealists did not die with the official demise of the movements and their subsequent museumification, the arts of the sixties did not end with the commercialization and the trivialization of some of their forms. There was also an important difference between the European artists between the wars and the Americans of the sixties, and that was the intrinsic practicality of Americans. The Europeans — with a few notable and much despised exceptions, like Salvador Dali — preferred suicide to adaptation, but this was certainly not the case with Americans, the sturdy descendants of practical inventors, garage-experimenters and traveling salesmen: the true children of the 20th century.

El Abuelo (Grandpa), 1985, acrylic, nickel, micarta, brass, photo, laminated acrylic, 2" x 3.75". Collection of Charlotte Hernandez Mann.

When Tom Mann set out to make jewelry for sale, he saw himself as a craftsman and a small-business man. In college he studied technical theater, set design and lighting, and supported himself by making jewelry and selling it in shops along the New Jersey shore. At some point, he raised money from his friends to open a store. For every $50 they lent him, he would give them back either $70 worth of jewelry or $60 in cash. All of them took jewelry. Tom opened a gallery and a health-food store. Such combinations do not seem particularly startling now, but they were quite so back then. Today, health food is a multi-billion-dollar business, and psychedelic-inspired jewelry of the era has become collectable. Still, it is to Tom's credit that he does not make a big deal out of being in the avant-garde. His sense of "art" was a later development.

AEPI 27, 1982, photo-collage pin commission, bronze, brass, silver, laminated acrylic, found objects, 2" x 3.5". Collection of Toni Passon.

When I ask him if hippies reinvented the body, making it possible to wear expressive jewelry that revealed something of one's beliefs, Tom agrees and defines the period as a "time for the liberation of everything it meant to be human — and everyone went out to test it." The "human" aspect of this activity was self-evident in those days. Tom was a spiritual seeker.

When I press him to define his art, he talks instead about Sufism, Zen, Eastern religions, and the need to "explode convention." During the war in Vietnam, he sought conscientious-objector status, and received moral support from the Quakers in his home state of Pennsylvania. He eventually developed a personal moral philosophy, intimately connected to his art and to the choices he makes on its behalf. He recalls some kind of Sufi graduation ceremony where the initiate is taken to a courtyard and shown an abstract object meant to open his "doors of perception."

As an itinerant jeweler, Tom traveled from fair to fair in the summer. Each August he rented space in a friend's shop in San Francisco's North Beach. He met an extraordinary number of people for whom he was a kind of occasional shaman. He made enough money to support himself, but barely enough. Such a theatrical existence was, doubtless, amusing and experientially fraught, but it must have also been exhausting. While selling his hippie jewelry, both his entrepreneurial mind and his artistic yearning kept searching for better solutions.

Tom at the workbench.

Mining the finds at Sky Parts, Winter Park, FL. Mann discovered this surplus outlet in 1972 after exhibiting at the Winter Park Arts Festival; it became the primary source of "found objects" in the Techno-Romantic design vocabulary.

"I always combined the business person with the artistic person," he says.

The path to work that was unmistakably his led through a long apprenticeship of imitating his teachers' work and borrowing designs. "By the mid-seventies I had my own style," he says, "but it wasn't until the mid-eighties that I began making distinctive, original work."

The defining moment came in 1982, when he began using objects foraged from surplus warehouses in Orlando, Florida. "The stuff came from the detritus of the space program, bits and pieces from Cape Canaveral, machine parts, old linotypes. I put these things together into a new system of jewelry."

The found objects came together in shapes that were both original and touchingly "human," somehow. Tom had found, in a specific American context, what the dadaists had once discovered at the very dawn of the mechanical age. He did not yet call his style "Techno-Romantic," his current trademark name for his objects, but he knew that he had found his voice.

A real test followed shortly thereafter. Focusing on his new pieces, he had neglected making and selling his bread-and-butter items, and was broke. He drove to the Milwaukee Lakefront Festival, a renowned showcase for crafts, taking with him only the new work.

"I wasn't going to eat until I sold something," he tells me.

He sold everything. And won a prize.

The foraging for found materials, and the painstaking process of assembling them, was not very profitable. Each piece was unique, interesting, an unmistakable Thomas Mann piece, but he was still unknown. The venues for showing art jewelry were also quite limited. There were no galleries specializing in this kind of art. Today, he says, "there are fifteen galleries that focus on contemporary metalwork."

But in the early eighties, jewelry was still considered a folk craft, and rarely "art."

Chamber Heart Necklace, 1994, bronze, silver, aluminum, 2" x 2.5".

He had found a style that he first called "Heartwear," because one of his recurrent motifs was the human heart, and then, rather prolixly, "Future Primitive Jewelry Objects" and "Para-Normal Jewelry Objects." None of these labels stuck, possibly because they didn't quite strike a euphonious note. In the end he came up with "Techno-Romantic," which was brief and descriptive of precisely what the objects intended.

Tom is quick to explain that "romantic" has little to do with "romance," that it is used in the sense of "human," in opposition to and in conjunction with "technical." The label is felicitous, indeed; it expresses our human dilemma at

Face Pins (group), 1986, silver, bronze, brass, laminated acrylic, 1" x 2".

a time when the very definition of what it is to be human is changing under the pressure of technology. As time speeds up and the technological future makes increasing demands on us, the past becomes more important, whether in the form of photographs or found objects. Even the past represented by fragments of now-obsolete technology, such as parts of linotype machines or discarded space junk, becomes oddly "human" when brought within the frame of a heart, a hand or a crafted box. This human crossroads between an amnesiac future and a nostalgic past found a satisfactory expression for Tom in his Techno-Romantic creations.

But Tom was himself at a crossroads between art and business. To make any money at his art, he had to sell a lot of it. To sell a lot of it, he had to put it into production. There was no question of backtracking to old proven crowd-pleasers, but neither did he intend to starve.

Glow in My Heart Pin, 1997, nickel, bronze, brass, glow-in-the-dark acrylic, 1" x 2.5".

Fly Like a Dove Pin, 1996, from the *Play Pin Collection,* bronze, brass, cast acrylic resin, 2.5" x 1.25".

There is something proudly self-made and solidly American about Tom. He admits that he may have gotten some of his skill from his father, who was a machinist. As a boy, Tom was a "kit-basher," which, he explains, is when you take a model car, for instance, and you "bash" it together with a toy tank, to make a new machine. He was also a big collector of everything, especially baseball cards. I imagine that growing up in a small Pennsylvania town in the 1950s is a perfect beginning for an American surrealist. At the same time, such beginnings are not the recipe for idleness. Writers who have grown up dreaming in such genuine American environments preferred drinking themselves to death rather than admitting defeat when their productivity declined. There is something hard and unforgiving about a "good" American childhood.

This is perhaps why, despite his success, Tom seems compelled to defend the artist-as-businessman. He invokes Picasso, a great artist and no slouch when it came to business. This feeling of residual guilt is not entirely the work of a Lutheran work ethic. I remember quite well the vehemence of a certain rhetoric of purity in the now-mythical late sixties. An artist, the saw went, was a pure creature who thought only of the higher verities and never dirtied his hands with filthy lucre. Around the same time, there circulated another distinction, that between art and craft. If the silliness of the materialistically innocent artist vanished as soon as Andy Warhol made his first million, the second myth wasn't so easy to dispel. I sense that Tom is still struggling with it. He refers to his craft as an "orphan of the art world."

This may have been even truer in the seventies and early eighties, but Tom himself has had quite a bit to do with the respectability gained by the craft since then.

1990

Tom found the solution to his survival dilemma in abandoning the time-consuming scavenging for found objects. Instead of spending weeks digging through bins of surplus, he started producing work that "looked like it was found." Eureka! It was a design leap. It was also an interesting solution from an artistic point of view. By asking himself the question of what exactly was "the serendipitous quality" of the found objects, he was able to generate series of objects, as well as pursue ideas through several transformations, without fear of running out of stuff. Producing "found" simulacra was also an interesting cultural comment in an age where nothing is what it seems to be. The appropriation by television of all the idealistic imagery of the sixties has put everything under the sign of irony. Tom admits quite freely that the collage-style of MTV has helped popularize his jewelry, by making his objects easier to understand.

At the beginning of his successful transformation, Tom made another fateful decision. He decided to stick by an earlier resolution to work exclusively in nonprecious materials.

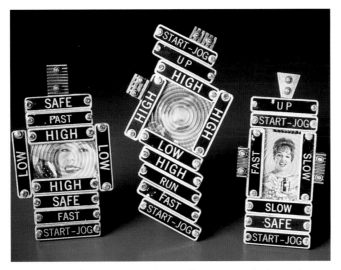

START JOG collection, 1987, photo-collage pin, acrylic, brass, aluminum, photo, instrument tags found at Boeing Surplus in Seattle, 1.75" x 2.75". Collection of the artist.

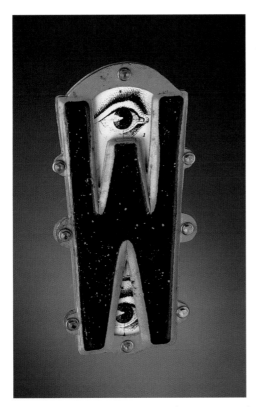

License Plate Pin Series, 1997–2000, aluminum or steel, acrylic, brass, antique photo, average 1.75" x 3".

Thomas Mann Gallery, exterior.

Thomas Mann Gallery, interior.

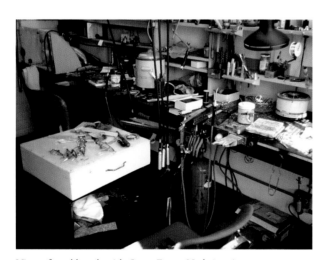

View of workbench with *Space Frame Neckpieces* in progress.

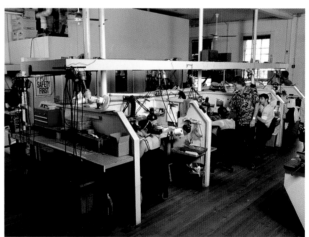

Production studio.

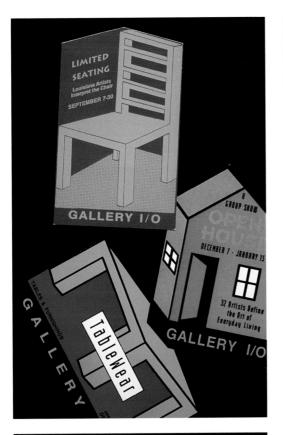

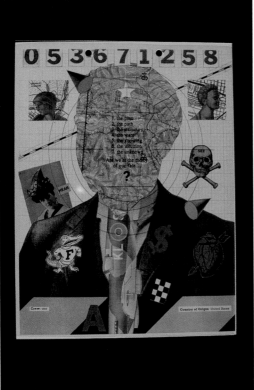

Gallery I/O graphics designed by Thomas Mann. ABOVE LEFT: mailers.
ABOVE RIGHT: Postcard mailer, *Veggie & Fruit Group,* 1992, acrylic, bronze,
brass, silver, found objects, 4" x 6". LEFT: Page from the catalog for
Collage/Assemblage show, 1991.

"I had two ways to go. I could go the precious route or the nonprecious route. The precious route: gold, precious stones, colored stones. Preciousness. The nonprecious route: silver, bronze, copper, plastic, stainless steel, found objects. The nonprecious route is low-cost; there is no concern about security. I was, and still am, more concerned with imagery and expression than with valuable objects. I am also still enough of a socialist to want my work to be available to everybody."

When I suggest that he should call his art and philosophy "The Nonprecious Path," he agrees enthusiastically for a brief moment, then reconsiders. He is loath to cut himself off from any possibility. He confesses also that he is now, in the new century of the new millennium, at another crossroads.

Crossroads are endemic in the lives of artists, no matter how well-regarded they may be by their contemporaries. "A career is just a series of comebacks," some cranky old actor said, and it's still true. For Tom, this particular crossroads comes in the wake of many career successes. He operates a small production workshop and gallery in New Orleans, on Magazine Street. His trademark is now widely known and his jewelry collected by connoisseurs and sought after by lovers of fine objects. Tom is also a bit of a guru, in demand for lectures on art and business. He

Commissioned collection for L.A. Eyewear, 1986-88, carved acrylics, micarta, bronze, brass, silver. Modeled by Deirdre Donchian, Lisa Poore and Helma Mezey, 1986-88.

has been the subject of articles in the professional media and is credited with elevating the field of contemporary metalwork. He has received commissions for large sculptures derived from his small designs.

Oddly enough, his success is also the source of his problems. Imitators have sprung up like mushrooms after the rain. (This is not an idle comparison: Tom himself compares his inspiration to a "well," and admits having hundreds of ideas he can

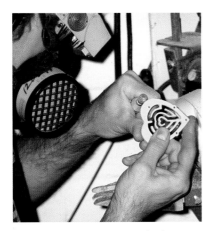

Tom carving *Heart Maze Pin* body.

The finished component.

Heart Maze Pin, 1998, micarta, bronze, acrylic, 2" x 2.5".

draw from it.) True appreciators of Thomas Mann work can easily tell his pieces from those of his imitators, but unknowing businesses display the copyists right alongside the original.

One solution for Tom is to begin working in precious metals, thus abandoning some of his populist views. After all, he explains, the "great artists of the Renaissance made beautiful things with gold." "Sure," I say, "but they made them for popes and kings." Point well taken. Tom grimaces.

Another solution is to make a transition to larger, sculptural works and to design for architects. Tom reflects back to his college days as a theater major and smiles ruefully. Everything comes around, eventually.

Tom does not dwell long on the difficulties. He sees them as opportunities for creative redefinition. He struggles with the label of "jeweler," for instance, preferring to call himself "an artist working in the medium of jewelry," a distinction that is all but lost to my ear. He has proven that jewelry, once thought of as an indulgence of the rich, has a social mission. Since the days of hippies, his work has attempted to be something more than just decorative. It is evident, at least to me, that he is an artist — and a jeweler. In his talk, Tom moves deftly between philosophy and shoptalk, between art and business, between the city and the country, and between the archaic and the technological. He wears a number of hats. He is a prestidigitator and a circus artist. It is not difficult to catch him swinging from one area to another, from one guise to another. He seems to be perpetually in the process of trading personae. This activity is both a professional and a generational hazard, but it keeps him vibrating.

Thomas Mann is in the process of giving an illustrated lecture about his work to new employees. The young apprentices are seated on surreal chairs, covered with plexiglass under which are trapped plates and forks. I sit gingerly, a bit afraid that the plexiglass will break and I will be impaled on the fork. Even someone disinclined to portraiture might take note of the fact that here is someone who wants to be helpful to the portraitist, ready to provide contexts and explanations, but not above impaling his observer.

How dangerous is Thomas Mann?

He has just put in a seemingly wrong slide. He says, "Ooops!" and clicks it off. Everyone laughs. In the slide, several naked folks, Tom among them, were standing on a rock above a lake, looking about to dive in.

"Nobody wears clothes on the island!" Tom explains. "We were burying treasure."

The island, Vinalhaven, off the coast of Maine, is where Tom summers. "It's where the naugah go to hide," chimes in Paige, one of his collaborators and his wife. She has doubtlessly heard this lecture before and is there to provoke him to spontaneity. Later, she asks him about the significance of his heart-in-hand image, one of the most familiar motifs of his jewelry design. "Part of my design vocabulary, nothing more," Tom says, deftly steering away from any psychological explanation.

The treasure about to be plunged into the 55-degree water of the quarry lake on Vinalhaven was a box containing jewelry, including a neckpiece Tom had created specifically for this occasion. This was one of a number of treasure boxes that were going to be hidden within the four elements of Water, Air, Earth and Fire. The year was 1995 and Tom's idea was to immerse and expose this jewelry to the four elements and then uncover it in the year 2000, in a new millennium. Each box contained ten strips of different metals, and the idea was to see what effects each medium of burial would have on them. Tom's idea had excited a number of his artist friends who added their own objects to the boxes. The symbolic time capsules eventually involved ten artists and twenty locations. Some of the locations were quite exotic, such as the tailgunner seat of a fighter plane at the Pima Air and Space Museum in Arizona. As the process of creating content for the boxes unfolded, the project became increasingly personal for Tom. The "Boise Box," for instance, intended for earth burial, was dedicated to the memory of one of his friend's "walks in the wilderness" and to other coincidences and connections having to do with the

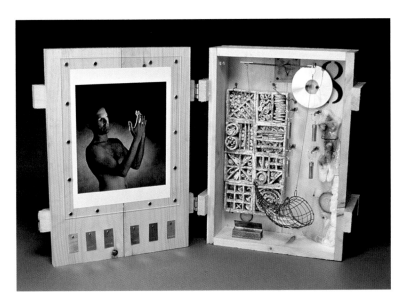

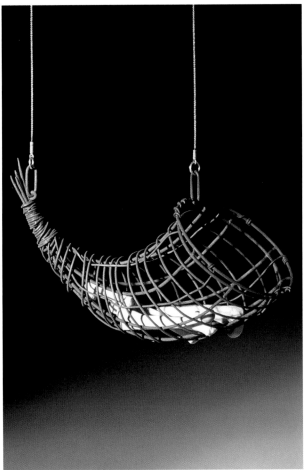

Burial Box No. 8 and *Cornucopia* neckpiece from the *OXIDATION/BURIAL* project. Burial site: Derby, MS, 1996. Neckpiece: silver, brass, bones, 5"x 4". Box: 20" x 5".

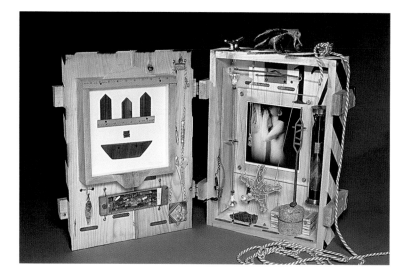

Box No. 17 and *Starfish* neckpiece from the *OXIDATION/BURIAL* project. Burial site: Big Pine Shoal, 10 miles east of Big Pine Key, FL, depth 45', 1997. Neckpiece: steel, paint, aluminum, 5"Dia; box: 14" x 20" x 5". ABOVE RIGHT: *Box No. 17* burial team, left to right: Tom, Carol Munder, John Martini, Terry Thomas. BOTTOM RIGHT: Tom and Terry diving *Box No. 17* to its interment site inside Terry's *Artificial Reef* sculpture.

town of Boise. As the project grew, so did its explicative armature and its rhetoric. Each burial was well documented. There are plans for an exhibition of the uncovered objects.

This small saga of the "Oxidation/Burial Project" and its cogent, though light-hearted presentation, are a near-perfect capsule of Thomas Mann, working artist and businessman. The handsome, middle-aged man delivering his standard philosophical lecture before new employees, who does not mind showing a naked, but "art-meaningful" slide of himself, was at ease with his self-image. Everything was on this slide: a hippie island, a philosophy of nature, a penchant for symbolic gestures, certain ideas about art, the cult of community, and American optimism. And everything was also in the presentation of the slide, with its slight awkwardness and the careful pedagogy directed at the employees of the small art factory. I had the feeling that three decades of American life had been carefully compressed within the brief flash of the "wrong" slide. What Tom had just "flashed through" was the trajectory of an artist from the socially active, "naked" early seventies to the entrepreneurial fin-de-siècle-cum-new-millennium.

There was an edge of satire in the whole enterprise. Time capsules are about as kitsch as our self-important culture gets. The time-capsule fad, which started in the 1950s under the threat of nuclear annihilation, embodied our worst tastes. If our civilization does indeed perish and future creatures unearth these objects, they will laugh themselves to death. Every small town in America has stuffed its capsule with Hallmark-like sentiments. Quite wisely, Tom decided to dig up his capsules as soon as the symbolic dateline was crossed. The project was a commentary on millennial hysteria, not an address to the future. Still, there was enough ambiguity to make even this reading tenuous. Doubtlessly, a slight smirk played over the operation. Tom clicked off the slide too fast for me to see if any of the naked people burying the treasure-trove in the quarry were wearing jewelry.

Do naked people need jewelry?

Jewels have always seemed to me slightly evil carriers of secret messages and, possibly, poisons. The Dumas brothers' novels spilled over with jewelry capable of seducing a musketeer, poisoning a helpless lover, hiding the message of a traitor, adorning evil men and women with secret powers, and ending a charming story by enclosing the main characters within a marriage ring. History is full of the poison rings of the Borgias, the ankle bracelets of slave girls (I liked those!), and the significantly arranged brooches of Mata Hari. The Bible trades blood for jewels and vice-versa from one story to another. Wealth and jewels were synonymous in the days when treasure chests were the main means for storing wealth. My own people, the Jews, had often been compelled to hoard gold against evil times. Our Rachels crossed borders laden with bracelets and anklets wound tightly so they wouldn't jingle as they walked. Gypsy women carried the entire wealth of the tribe wound around their necks, and they still do.

To my mind, jewelers were meticulous and unsentimental men who developed clocks and mechanisms. With their loupes screwed into one eye socket, they surveyed the miniature worlds of precious stones and metals and crafted the hair-triggers of time and weaponry.

Ritual and magical traditions always involved jewelry. Alchemy was the daughter of metalsmithing. Charlatans worked the field right alongside real seekers, giving retroactive charm to all the heads lost in the process. The ultimate adornment of the criminal was the rope around the neck. Oddly enough, the preciousness of the metal determined its virtue. The obverse of virtue was vice. Stealing a gold necklace could earn you a rope necklace. The shapes were similar. In fairy tales, paths paved with gold and precious stones led to dragons' lairs. Fingers were cut off for the rings on them.

Tom does not belie these stereotypes. They are useful to him, like all legends about a craft that is both versatile and articulate.

Jewelry has always carried the burden of communication. In the beginning, it was intended to signal status and it was as rigid as the lines it drew. A crown, a royal ring, a gold breastplate or a precious neckpiece were instantly legible to the wearers' subjects. The adornments were always proportional to wealth,

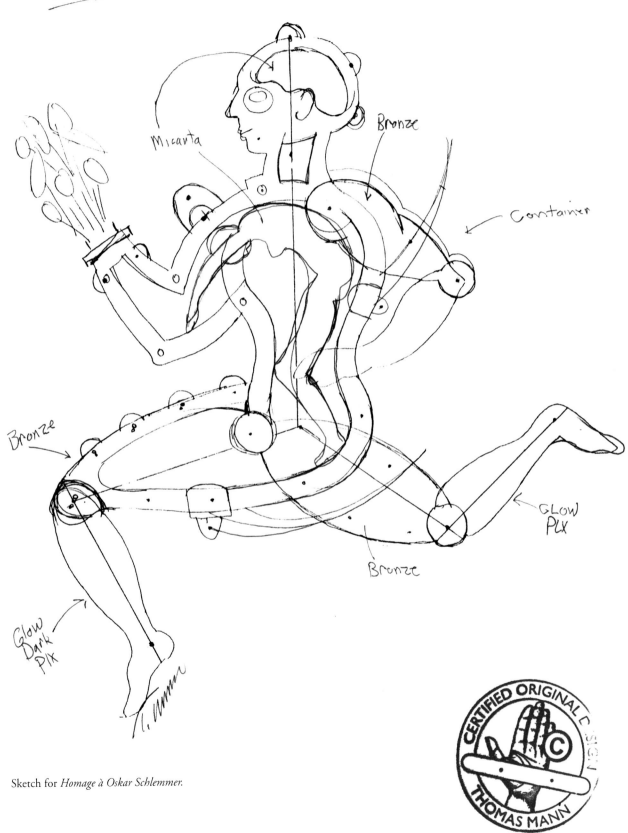

"Homage a Oskar Schlemmerer"

Micarta

Bronze

Container

Bronze

Bronze

GLOW
PLX

Glow
Dark
PLX

Sketch for *Homage à Oskar Schlemmer.*

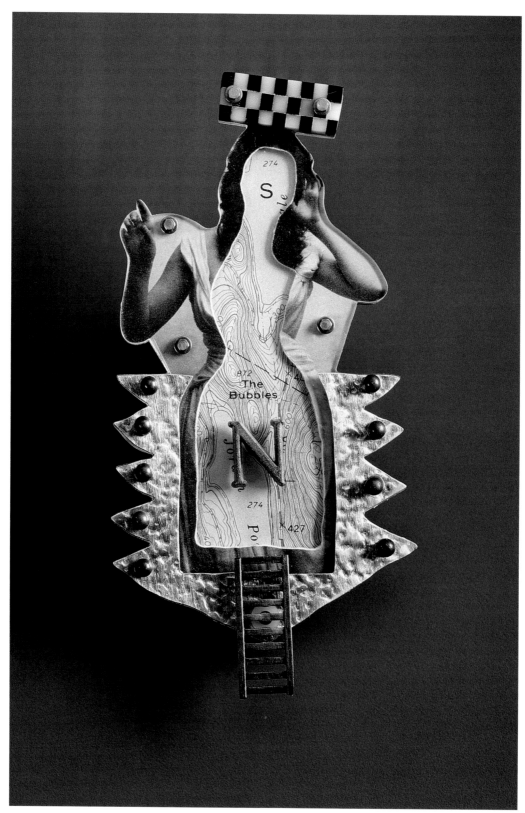

DaDa Diva, 1991, silver, brass, bronze, photo, acrylic, laminated acrylic, 2" x 4".

House of Work, 1978, box construction with removable brooch, wood, glass, acrylic, nickel, zinc, paper, antique tintype, found objects, 18"H x 14"W x 5"D.

Homage à Cornell, 1987, box construction, wood, glass, acrylic, paper, found objects, 16"H x 14"W x 4"D. This box is a salute to Joseph Cornell. It contains a wearable, removable pin modeled on the bird objects Cornell included in many of his pieces.

though certain designs belonged exclusively to royalty and could not be reproduced no matter how rich one happened to be. The language of ornament is as ancient and as complex as language itself and, like the language we speak, it ranged from the sacred to the frivolous, from the awe-inspiring to happy babble. Bauble and babble are kindred notions.

Oddly enough, the German writer whom Tom does not in the least resemble was one of the reasons why I decided to attempt this literary portrait. I had been reading a new translation of *Faust* and pulling my exasperated hair over the excruciatingly slow pace of Mann's prose, its insistence on every stolid bourgeois detail of his characters' tormented Lutheran psychology. The sin of which Faust is guilty — and of which Mann wanted to rid himself — was precisely the agility of character capable of transcending a narrow morality to become something else, including its opposite. The net effect of reading *Faust* was to make me wish fervently for an escape to surrealism, whimsy, joie-de-vivre, or any other place where one's actions are not subjected to such maddening analysis and guilt. That's when Thomas Mann, the jeweler, showed up.

There are any number of differences and resemblances between Mann the writer and Mann the jeweler, and only a surrealist would attempt to compare them. So here we go. Both Mann the writer and Mann the jeweler were born Lutheran. Both of them tell stories. Mann the writer, born in Germany, was made to feel the weight of his religion by the rise of pagan Hitlerism and by the need to suppress his homosexual desires. Mann the jeweler was born in America and was liberated in the 1960s by hippie paganism and its pacifist-surrealist ideals. The stories the two men tell couldn't be more different. Mann the writer tells about human beings caught in the vicious grip of history and psychology. Mann the artist-jeweler tells techno-romantic stories meant to let people out of those cages. Writer Mann belongs

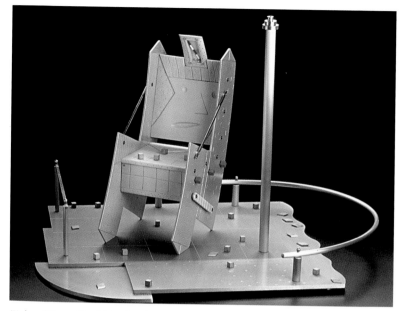

Techno-Throne No. 2 (platform), 1985, *Techno-Throne* series, micarta, aluminum, brass and acrylics, chair: 5" x 11" x 12"; platform: 16" x 16"; brooch: 1.75" x 2.5".

wholly to the first, dark half of the century. Jeweler Mann is a child of the second. Still, they have things in common. Both Manns are masters of detail. The writer's prose is crafted like a jewel from extremely precise observations. The jeweler is, by necessity, a man of detail. The effects of their attention to detail is quite different, though. One Mann's writerly detail is oppressive, leaving the reader little room to interpret and to dream. The other Mann's details are brought together for the purpose of creating paradoxical objects that invite interpretation and reverie. And one more thing: Mann the writer ended up living in exile in America, but never left Germany in his mind, with one exception. That exception was Venice, where a fleeting sense of liberty possessed him, only to end up punished by death. *Death in Venice* was an escape. Thomas Mann, the artist and craftsman, lives in New Orleans, the one North American city that can be compared to Venice. Is Thomas Mann, the American, an escaped wish of Thomas Mann the writer?

Techno-Throne No. 2 Brooch (platform), 1985, *Techno-Throne* series, micarta, brass, acrylics, photo, 1.75" x 2.5".

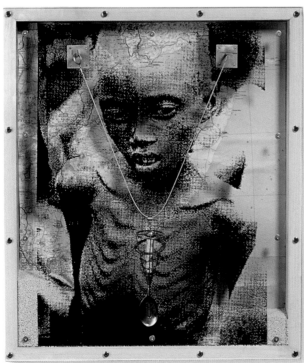

Food for Thought traveling exhibition, 1993. TOP: Installation view, Gallery I/O, New Orleans. BOTTOM LEFT AND RIGHT: *Food Is Not a Weapon,* 1993, *Space Frame Neckpiece,* silver, bronze, rice, 5.5"DIA.

Absurd question. Not unlike one of Tom's pieces. Here, for instance, is a self-portrait in brass, bronze, micarta, photo and laminated Lucite, in which Tom, encased by wheels and fastened to the frame, peers through uneven lenses at the viewer and makes the thumbs-up gesture. There is little to feel victorious about, given the self-created trap he has made for his image, but the piece is funny, a kind of illustration of the folk saying, "You made your bed and now you lie in it." When I ask Tom about it, he says with a grin, "I tried to give myself the same kind of treatment I've given others."

Indeed. The ability to reinvent himself is one of Tom's best and most American qualities. Such reinvention is only possible if one remains open to the spontaneous and unexpected. One of my favorite works of Tom's is the pin-up

Self-Portrait (thumbs up), 1995, from the *Self-Portrait Brooch* series, brass, bronze, micarta, photo, laminated acrylic, 2.75" x 4.5". Collection of the artist.

series, which he created by collaging a virgin pack of pin-up cards — a gift from a friend — into a series of pins. This is possibly the sexiest and funniest of Tom's many photo-maulings. The pin-up models look happily constrained by the many frames Tom has made for them. Other people from the past look hopelessly encased and "mechanized" by fragments of late-20th-century machinery.

As I leaf through the folder of slides, I chance a few glances at Tom himself, preoccupied with a sheaf of papers behind a cluttered desk. In the studio below, his dozen employees, now properly lectured to and hopefully baffled, are assembling designs, surrounded by shelves, drawers, and barrels full of Tom's signature materials. The mastermind is frowning, thinking of crossroads. Or trying to

OPPOSITE: *Ltd. Edition Teapot Necklace*, 1997, silver, brass, bronze, nickel, micarta, laminated acrylic, centerpiece: 3" x 2.5". The tea container in this piece removes to become a functional tea infuser. Edition of 25.

figure out how to take over the world using everyday objects. Or considering what a complicated relationship his hero, Marcel Duchamp, had with the poet Mina Loy. Or considering lunch. In New Orleans, lunch is an art.

Attempting the portrait of a living artist is a hazard-fraught enterprise. It's bad enough when the artist resists explication and refuses to collaborate in elucidating his work, as was the case when Frank O'Hara wrote his monograph on Jackson Pollock. It's worse when the portraitist takes on someone who loves to explicate the work and is not loath to philosophize, mythologize and embellish, as was the case when Picasso painted Gertrude Stein. "I don't look like that," Stein is reputed to have said. "You will," Picasso told her.

I am trying to capture Thomas Mann, a jeweler who explicates like Stein and labors like Pollock. Alas, Thomas Mann is elusive. He is, as Lucian Blaga said in a famous poem, "hidden in the light." The fertility of his imagination and the open celebration of his artistic sources are clear in his work, but the artist is still in shadow. The dada-surrealist art that has provided Tom with his imaginative license is only part of the story. The hippies are another part. His pieces sometimes look like a lament for the natural world, pinned and imprisoned by bits of circuitry and plastic. At other times, the formal richness of the materials and the prettiness of the shape seem effusive and adoring. This ambiguity is also the history of a generation, a history Tom has internalized and about which he will always philosophize. Without crossroads he'd be lost.

Is my face red?, 1991-96, from the *Pin-Up Pin* series, acrylic, bronze, brass, silver, found objects, vintage pin-up postcards, 2.5" x 5". Collection of Rimas VisGirda.

Sketchbook page exhibited in "Drawing the Lines: Selections from Jewelers' Sketchbooks," March 2000, curated by Gail M. Brown for The Society of Arts and Crafts, Boston, MA.

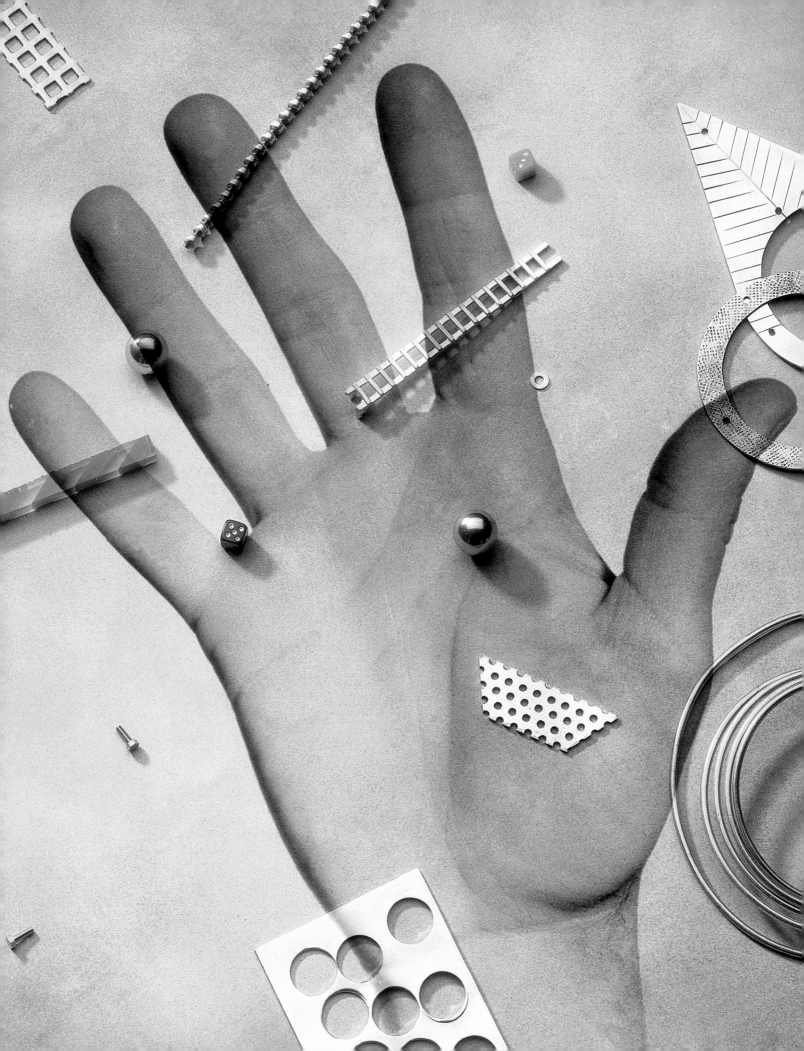

PORTFOLIO
THE ARTIST'S VOICE

Thomas Mann

THE GOLDEN AGE

"I BELIEVE WE HAVE LIVED THROUGH A GOLDEN AGE IN AMERICAN CRAFT WORK. WHAT has taken place in the contemporary craft movement over the past 50 years is special and important, and will be looked back on with a kind of reverence. I believe this Golden Age is now past and the movement will wait for its renewal some decades hence.

The arts and crafts movement that began in the 1890s experienced the same development and decline. At its height, between 1910 and 1920, the designers and makers of this era influenced a range of products that became commonplace in the American marketplace. The principle design motifs of the movement influenced the development of art deco and, later, modernist designers. By the mid 1920s, the movement dissipated into broad acceptance as a design system.

Our contemporary craft movement is now, after a dynamic and powerful period, experiencing those same conditions of absorption into the mainstream. American craft artists have raised the level of consciousness of the American public; the look, style and materials of the craft world are now 'mined' by mass marketers, including some of the best and most popular. But their product is made 'off-shore,' in Third World countries with inexpensive labor. This is good and bad. Bad because it dilutes the general public perception of value relative to price. Good because it elevates the work of the *true* craft

ABOVE: 1995

OPPOSITE: Photo layout for resume brochure.

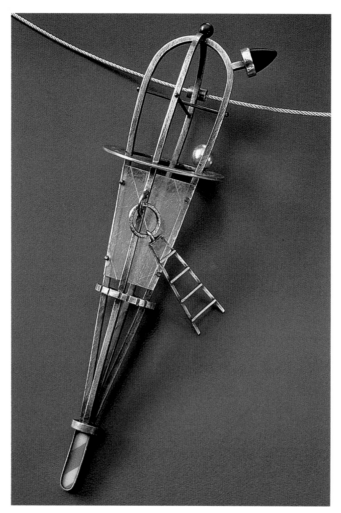

Do You Believe in Luck – Or Is It Just Fate?, 1992, *Space Frame Neckpiece* series, silver, brass, bronze, laminated acrylic, black onyx, fiberglass, aluminum, 1.5" x 5.5".

artist for those who know the difference, those who still value the important exchange that takes place when they acquire work directly from the artists who make it, or through their representatives in stores, shops and galleries.

I am enormously fortunate to have participated in this incredible period in the American craft movement. And while the heady days of the field's development may be past, we continue to enjoy the rewards of an appreciative public who celebrate the work of the hand by supporting the artists who have chosen craft as their careers."

OPPOSITE: *Space Frame Brooches and Neckpiece,* 1992, silver bronze, brass, acrylic, black onyx, fiberglass, beach pebbles, laminated acrylic. Left to right: 1.5" x 5.5", 1.5" x 4", 2" x 4".

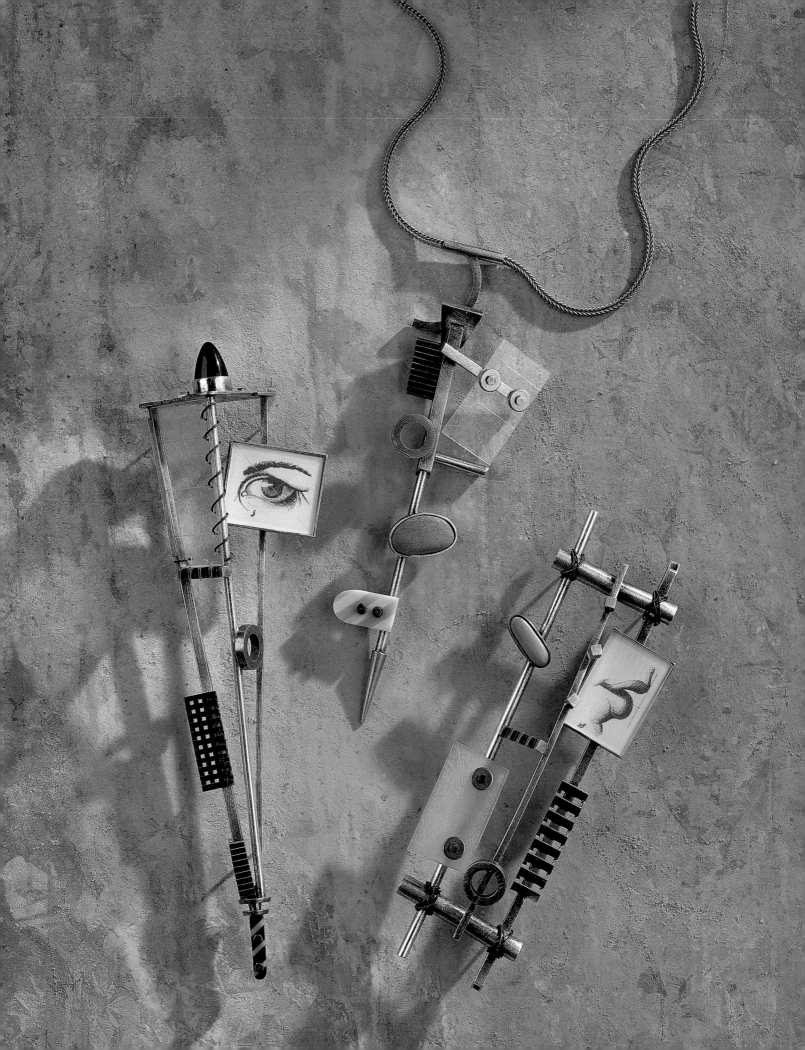

Cheerio Fetish Necklace, 1984, silver, brass, micarta, aluminum, copper, found objects, 24" long x 2.5" at widest point. Collection of Elizabeth A. Black.

Original Fetish Necklace, 1980, silver, brass, acrylic, aluminum dial, copper, found objects, 22" long. Collection of Eileen and Robert Miner.

Construct Stone Necklace, 1979, silver, brass, bronze, with rutilated quartz, 2" x 2.75". Collection of Eileen and Robert Miner.

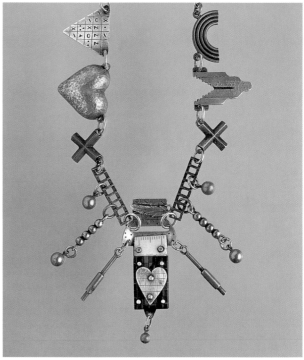

Fetish Necklace, 1986, silver, brass, bronze, laminated acryic, aluminum dial, copper, found objects. Collection of Linda Given.

"Some symbols are common denominators, archetypal glyphs that every culture on the planet intuitively understands. They've been around since human history began.

At Lascaux, in southwestern France, and among the rock outcroppings of the Australian outback, ancient artists, using their hands as masking, spit liquefied pigment onto the rock face, revealing the negative impression of their hands.

With hands we made our way in the world. With hands we took dominion over nature, for good or bad. The symbol of the hand appears in every cultural symbol index from the hand of Buddha in India to the Hand of Fatima (the thrice blessed daughter of Mohammed) used in amulets to ward off the evil eye. The very same hand appears in Semitic culture as the *Hamsa.* Techno-Romantic reinterprets this powerful symbol for the 21st century.

The heart is a trickster, a symbol with a secret meaning and purpose. Since the days of chivalry, when spiritual love was converted to amorous love, the heart has been the symbol of romance, specifically heterosexual romance. But the romantic love symbol thing is simply a PC cover for the fact that the heart form is really a powerful sexual symbol. Its shape is taken from a certain area of the female anatomy and has always been employed, though most folks don't know it, as a fertility symbol.

This is the core symbol of humanity, because although we are thinking, creative, imaginative beings, there is also within us a base animal instinct that drives us to procreate."

CERF Hand Pin, 1999, silver, brass, bronze, glow-in-the-dark acrylic, acrylic, 1.75" x 3". One of 30 hand-theme pieces made by artists as a fundraising project for the Craft Emergency Relief Fund.

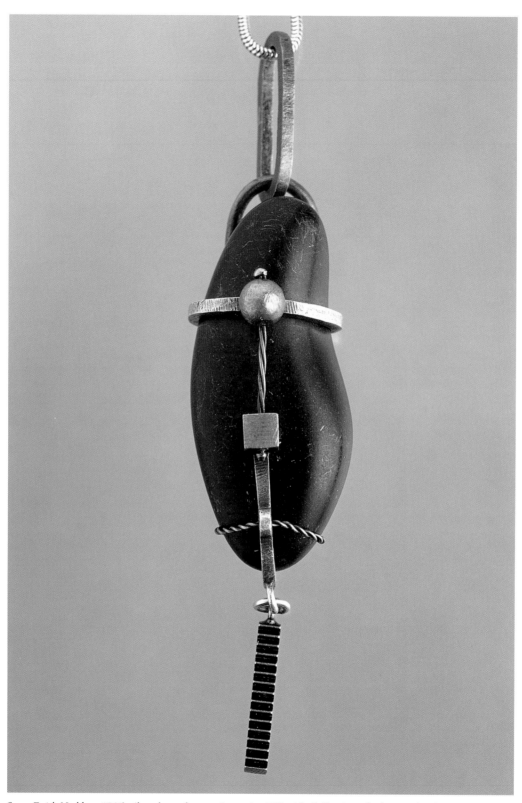

Stone Fetish Necklace, 1996, silver, brass, bronze, iron wire, 75" x 3". Collection of Eileen and Robert Miner.

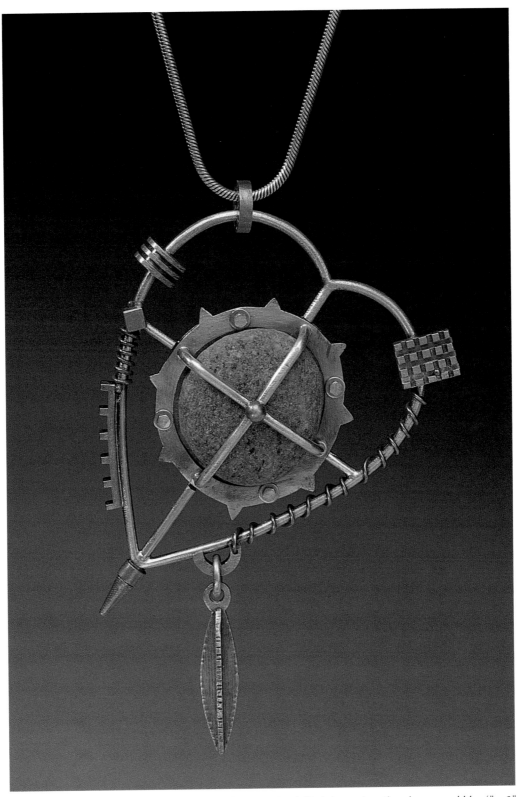

Between a Rock and a Heart Place, 1996, from the *Stone Fetish Neckpiece* series, silver, bronze, pebble, 4" x 3". Collection of Sandra Webster.

Spiral Fetish Brooch, 1997, silver, patinated brass, copper, bronze, pebble, steel, 2" x 6".

Stone Fetish Neckpiece, 1994, silver, bronze, beach pebble, 4" x 3".

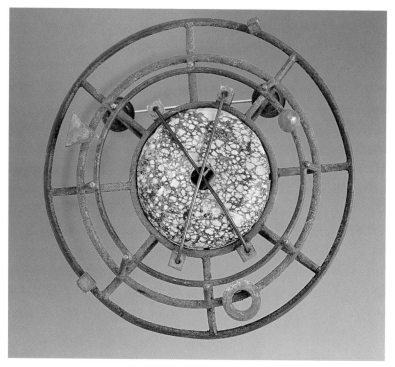

Rusted Space Frame Stone Fetish Brooch, 1997, steel, bronze, brass, turquoise. Collection of Beth Abrams.

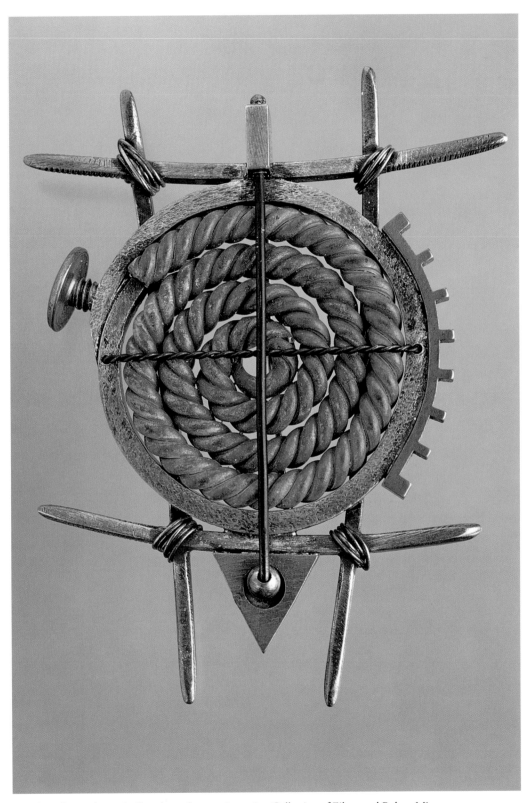

Spiral Fetish Brooch, 1995, silver, brass, bronze, iron wire. Collection of Eileen and Robert Miner.

"What is a collector? When do collectors become self-aware? And once they do, what is their collecting agenda?

Many collectors of my work don't realize that they are, in fact, 'collectors.' Fans become collectors when they realize that their acquisition behavior might have a purpose beyond feeding their hobby. They may begin to consider the secondary market for the works, or the opportunity to donate their collection to a museum and reap personal satisfaction, as well as tax benefits. Or perhaps they decide to pass the collection along as an inheritance.

Whatever the case might be, a relationship develops between the artist and his or her collectors. These people understand the nature of the support artists must have to do what they do. Throughout history, artists have depended on the sympathetic collector for support and sustenance.

I like to think of my collectors as a more egalitarian group than Picasso enjoyed. I made a decision in the late 1970s to make my work available to the widest audience possible by choosing nonprecious material and pricing the work for broad accessibility. Making the nonprecious precious is a kind of alchemy. Turning copper, brass, bronze, aluminum and steel into gold is a neat trick if you can manage it. I like to think that the philosophy and working dictums of Techno-Romantic are capable of producing this effect."

ABOVE: There's always a Rhodia graph paper pad in the artist's back pocket. This is where spontaneous ideas are preserved for future rumination. Pages are sometimes enlarged by photocopying, then reworked to become the plans for new work.

OPPOSITE: *Multi-Stone Fetish Necklace,* 1999, silver, bronze, brass, Montana agate, black onyx, hematite, rose quartz, red coral, yellow agate, carved Austrian crystal. Centerpiece: 1.5" x 3.25". Collection of Froma I. Zeitlin.

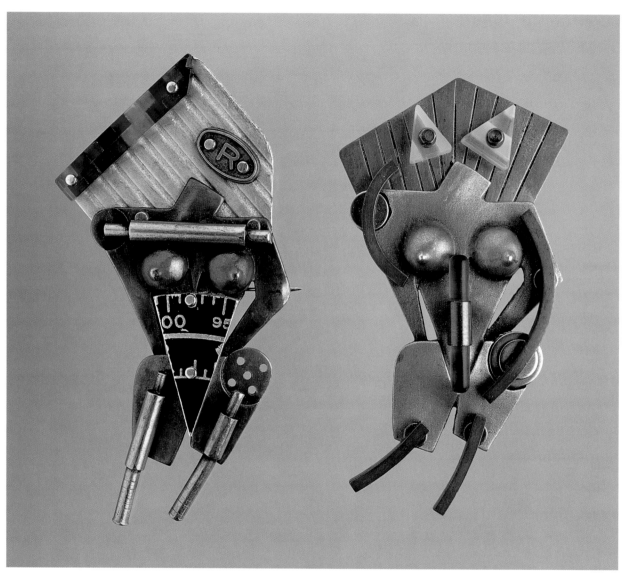

Collage Torso Pins, 1997, silver, brass, bronze, 1.5" x 2.25". Collections of Joyce Goodman and Bonnie Erickson.

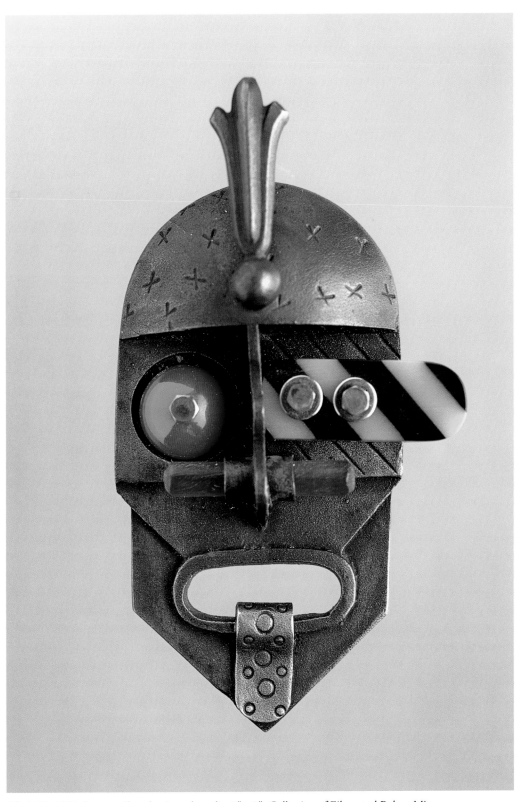

Mask Pin, 1989, bronze, silver, laminated acrylic, 1" x 2". Collection of Eileen and Robert Miner.

SHINY METAL VS. MATTE

"Stereotypes, the status quo, the common expectation, have always unnerved me.

I spent countless hours at the buffing wheel as an apprentice and young freelance professional, delivering that stereotypical highly polished surface. It was dirty, dangerous and boring, and I hated every moment of it. I thought about why people equate high polish with high quality; it probably has something to do with the ancient mystery of mirrors, since the first mirrors were polished metal surfaces.

But there had to be other surfaces within the palette of metal-finishing techniques that could imbue the final work with meaning and grace. I'd used steel wool to prepare surfaces for soldering and realized that I liked the look and feel of that surface. It wasn't long after this realization (around 1975) that I simply substituted the steel wool finish for the polished one.

This all fit in with my natural-metals philosophy. Life is oxidation. Everything on the planet is subject to its interaction with oxygen; we're all just burning up, slowly but surely. The polished surface on a piece of jewelry has many purposes. Besides delighting the eye and reflecting light and images it also slows down the oxidation process. By using finer and finer grits of polishing compounds, the jeweler in effect closes up the surface of the metal, changing the jagged porous surface to a tightly aligned pattern of molecules. This surface resists the penetration of the oxygen molecules, thus slowing down the chemical process of oxidation, commonly known as 'tarnishing.'

The matte finish I embraced so fervently leaves the metal open to oxidation. You can't stop it anyway: despite the polished surface, tarnishing will inevitably occur. Polishing metal is like trying to discover the Fountain of Youth, or using cosmetics and cosmetic surgery to prevent aging. You can polish a piece of silver or brass 'til it's shiny as a mirror, you can coat it with clear lacquer or resin in an attempt to prevent oxidation. But these changes are superficial. They won't stop the process, so why not just go with it? Why not employ it?

The terms I invented for my work — Heartware, Future Primitive, Para-Normal and finally Techno-Romantic Jewelry Objects — all convey the fact that though the

Starfish, 1984, photo-collage pin, brass, acrylic, antique photograph, bronze, 2.25"DIA. Collection of Bonnie Erickson.

pieces have a contemporary look, their appeal lies in their links to both past and future. The link to the past comes in the form of the patina, the artificial tarnishing that is delivered to the piece with chemical patinas and a steel wool finish. The people who own the work can maintain this finish themselves at any level of patination. They can let it get dark and old looking or keep it bright and new looking. They participate with me and with nature, enjoying their piece according to their own take on all of the above!"

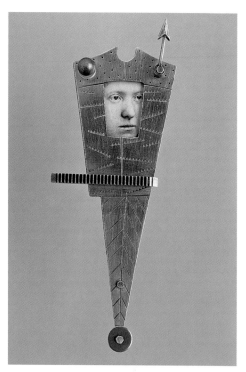

Delta, 1987, photo-collage pin, silver, brass, stainless steel, antique photograph, laminated acrylic. Collection of Marion Andrus McCollam.

Mother and Child, 1989, photo-collage pin, silver, brass, acrylic, laminated acrylic, stainless steel and photo, 1.25" x 2.75". Collection of Joyce Goodman.

Man with Hat and Fish, 1990, photo-collage pin, silver, brass, stainless steel, antique photograph, laminated acrylic. Collection of Elissa Topol and Lee Osterman.

All Day Ma Made Hay, 1990, photo-collage pin, bronze, silver, antique photograph. Collection of Elissa Topol and Lee Osterman.

I Am Waiting for Love to Tell Me When, 1976, photo-collage pin, brass, silver, found objects, tintype, laminated acrylic, 1.5" x 3".

Dreamscape, 1975, photo-collage pin, brass, acrylic, ivory, tintypes, paint, 2.5" x 3".

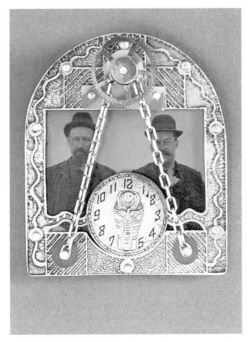

TickTock, 1978, photo-collage pin, photo-etched bronze, brass, silver, found objects, tintype, acrylic, paint, 2.25" x 3".

Blue Boy, 1975, photo-collage pin, brass, silver, found objects, tintype, laminated acrylic, paint, 1.5" x 3".

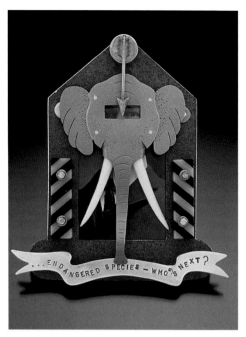

Endangered Species, Who's Next?, 1992, photo-collage pin, acrylic, steel, striped laminate, photo, nickel, brass, micarta, 2.5" x 4". Made for a Save the Elephants fundraising event at the Flying Shuttle in Seattle, WA.

Blue Girl, 1992, photo-collage pin, laminated acrylic, brass, silver, micarta, antique photograph, 2" x 3.5".

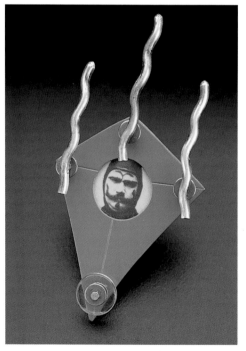

Green, 1986, photo-collage pin, acrylic, brass, silver, micarta, antique photograph, 1.5" x 3".

Devil in Green, 1988, photo-collage pin, acrylic, brass, nickel, paint, antique photograph, 1.25" x 2.75".

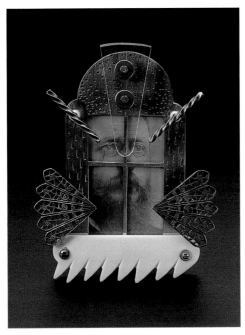

Herr Freud, 1983, photo-collage pin, acrylic, bronze, silver, micarta, antique photograph, 2" x 3.75".

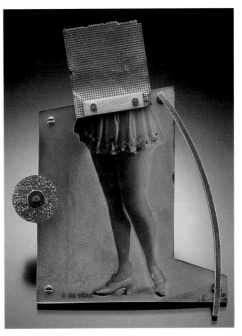

Dance, 1990, photo-collage pin, acrylic, nickel, postcard, silver, aluminum, 2" x 4".

STOP, 1984, photo-collage pin, acrylic, bronze, nickel, laminate, found objects, antique photograph, 1.75" x 3".

Boat, 1990, photo-collage pin with wall mounting, nickel, brass, laminated acrylic, antique photograph, acrylic, wood and rubber bands. Collection of the artist.

Endangered Species, Who's Next, 1977, photo-etched brass, bronze, found objects, tintype, paint, 2.25" x 2.25".

Hi-Ton Sisters, 1978, photo-collage pin triptych, aluminum, brass, acrylic, laminated acrylic, ivory, tintypes, found objects, paint, 1.5" x 5.5".

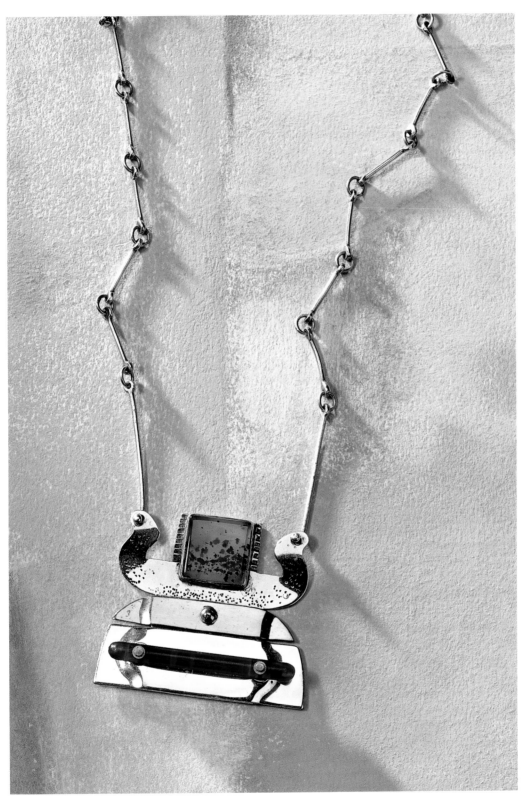

Landscape Pendant, 1975, silver, brass, acrylic with Montana agate. Collection of Eileen and Robert Miner.

"Artisans have been exhibiting their wares at fairs for thousands of years. It's nothing new, really. But I like to think the craft fairs and shows I've participated in since 1970 stand apart from those of the past.

I've had the good fortune to witness the development of the contemporary exhibition-and-marketing system from its infancy to its adulthood. At first, the field was inhabited primarily by teachers, who could exhibit only once or twice a year. Now, the sophisticated business management skills developed by many professional craft artists allow them to produce their work and still fly to ten or twenty distant exhibitions each year. Initially, artists displayed their products on folding tables or blankets on the ground; today, our ingenious trade-show booths come with sophisticated lighting and display mechanisms.

As for the artwork, I've witnessed ever-increasing creativity and inventiveness with materials and techniques. I've also watched, with growing personal anxiety, as the marketplace for craft has changed; derivative, imitative designs and competitive pricing tactics have replaced the fair play and respect of the early years. Despite this, the fairs still offer a wonderful opportunity for artists to interact with their audience and receive immediate feedback as they experiment with new ideas.

Fairs also provide the cash flow that keeps artists doing what they are here to do for all of us: enrich our lives with creativity and imagination, and deliver objects engorged with real human energy and meaning. I always tell the students who take my 'Design *for* Survival' courses that the objects we make are really only tangible symbols of the energy being exchanged with the patron. We put all our energy and creativity into the object through the process of realizing it. Patrons exchange their energy and creativity through the means of transaction (i.e., money) that they worked hard to acquire. This exchange relationship is unlike any other in the human experience.

Craft fairs have become the vehicle for this exchange. The show promoters who produce them, the artists who exhibit, and the public who attend and acquire have together created an environment that celebrates our humanity and creativity."

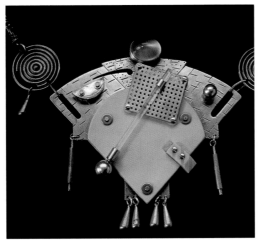

Delta, 1983, Construct series neckpiece, bronze, aluminum, brass, silver, laminated acrylic, micarta, moonstone, abalone, centerpiece: 5.5" x 4.5".

Collage Fetish Neckpiece, 1984, bronze, aluminum, brass, silver, striped laminated acrylic, 1.8" x 2.25".

Stone Construct Brooch, 1986, silver, brass, steel, Montana agate, moonstone, 2" x 4".

Stone Construct Neckpiece, 1986, silver, bronze, steel, Montana agate, hematite, 3" x 3.5".

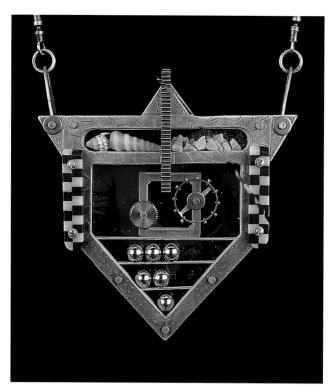

Collage Box Neckpiece, 1986, minerals, acrylics, brass, silver, photo, found objects, 4" x 4.5".

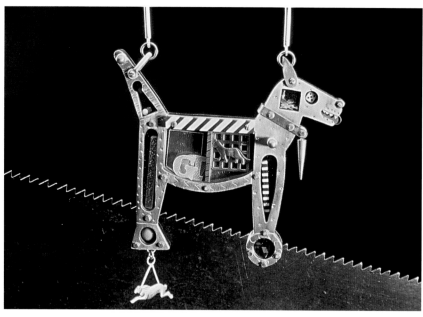

Dog Box Neckpiece, 1994, acrylics, brass, nickel, found objects, micarta, 4.5" x 4".

OPPOSITE: *Dog Box Necklace,* 1998, nickel, bronze, brass, found objects, acrylic, 2.5" x 3.5".

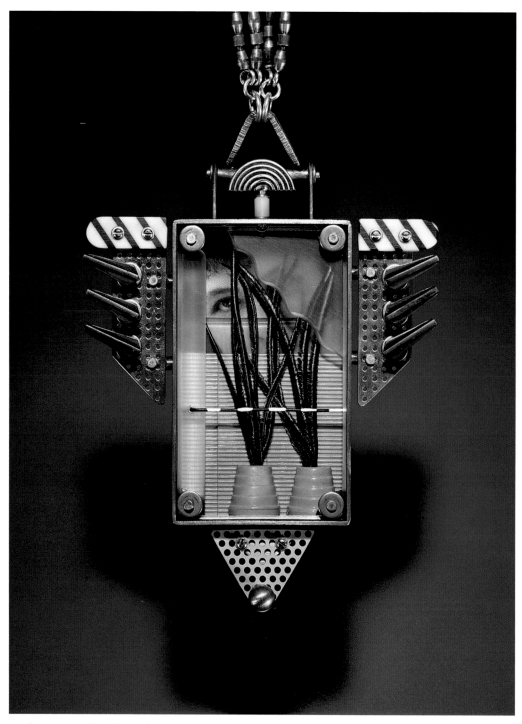

Feathers, 1988, collage box neckpiece, silver, brass, bronze, copper, found objects, antique photograph, 2.25" x 4".

Blue Girl, 1990, collage box neckpiece, silver, brass, bronze, copper, found objects, antique photograph, 3.25" x 4.75".

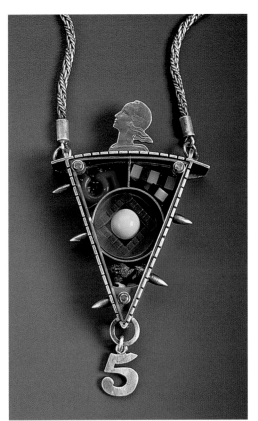

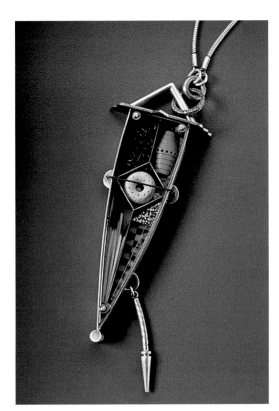

Collage Box Neckpieces, silver, brass, bronze, copper, found objects or objects fabricated to appear found. OPPOSITE: *Delta,* 1991, 2" x 4" and *Cross,* 1991, 1.75" x 4.5". ABOVE: *Donut,* 1991, 2.5" x 6". ABOVE RIGHT: *No. 5,* 1986, 2.5" x 3". Collection of the American Craft Museum. RIGHT: *Dice,* 1986, 2.5" x 3".

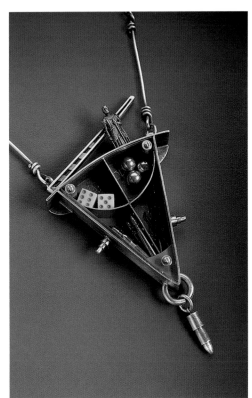

PLASTICS

"I was a kit-basher when I was a kid. A kit-basher takes parts from different model kits and assembles them into new 'morphed' (not a term we used then) objects. The front end of a car combined with the tail of a plane with a tank turret and rocket engines — something like that. I loved the glue because it held everything together. And this was before Super Glue! To make it work you had to be meticulous. My dad built me my own workbench next to his, but at my scale. He furnished the tools, but my brother Todd and I always snitched his as well.

Plastics were invented accidentally in the early 1800s, as a result of investigations with soap and cellulose. Eventually they became preferable, for many uses, to natural products. My youth was full of them. The fifties was the plastic decade. I remember the time my father accepted a contract to manufacture Blue Cross/Blue Shield desk placards for doctors' offices. He did it all in his basement shop so our house smelled like plexiglass for months. To this day the odor of acrylic solvent always takes me back to that time, when Todd and I had the job of pulling paper off precut slabs of plexiglass used to make the laminated signs. So, plastics …Techno-Romantic wouldn't exist without 'em."

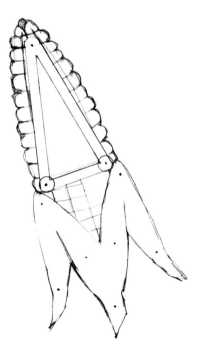

Opposite: *Veggie & Fruit Series,* 1992, acrylic, bronze, brass, silver, found objects, various dimensions. Collection of Susan Connelly Korenewski.

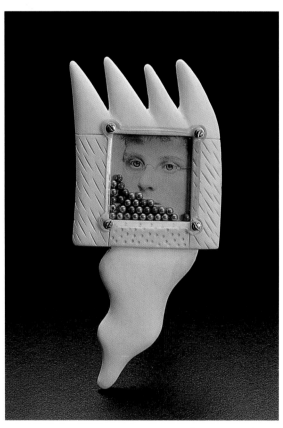

Micarta Pin series. ABOVE: *See,* 1992, acrylic, micarta, photo, brass, 2" x 3". ABOVE RIGHT: *Plaque Structure No. 3,* 1989, micarta, bronze, brass, acrylic, 2" x 3". RIGHT: *Compass,* 1992, acrylic, micarta, photo, brass, 1.75" x 4".

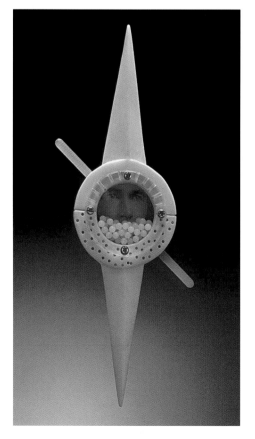

The JET Family at Home: JETman, JETwoman and JETbaby, 1985, carved micarta, brass, .75" x 2.75" for the adults. Design inspired by the graphic signage on the sides of engines on jet aircraft indicating safety zones to ground personnel.

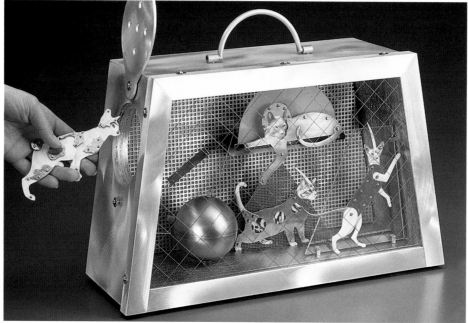

Cat Box, collage box sculpture with removable, wearable brooches, 1993, wood, aluminum, glass, silver, bronze, micarta, paper, acrylic, brooch size: average 2" x 4.5"; box :13" x 10" x 6".

OPPOSITE: *Bird Box Aviatrix,* collage box sculpture containing 16 removable, wearable bird brooches, 1989, wood, aluminum, glass, silver, bronze, micarta, paper, acrylic, brooch size: average 2" x 4.5"; box: 18" x 33" x 6". Collection of Charlie and Peg Bishop.

Insectarium, 1998, aluminum, glass, brass, Lucite, wood, 20"W x 25" x 12.5".

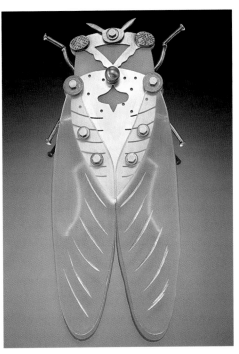

Cicada Pin, 1998, from the *Insectarium,* silver, glow-in-the-dark acrylic, brass, acrylic, 1.5" x 2.5".

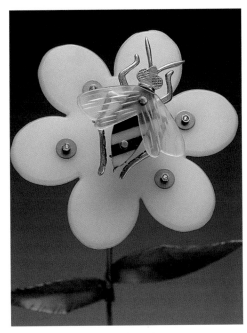

Bee Pin on Flower, 1998, from the *Insectarium,* silver, brass, acrylic, laminated acrylic, 1.5" x1.75".

Ladybird Beetle Pin, 1998, from the *Insectarium,* 1.25" x 1.75".

OPPOSITE: *Aquariatrix,* collage box sculpture with removable, wearable fish brooches, 1991, wood, aluminum, glass, silver, bronze, micarta, paper, acrylic, box: 22" x 26" x 6"; brooch size: average 2.5" x 3".

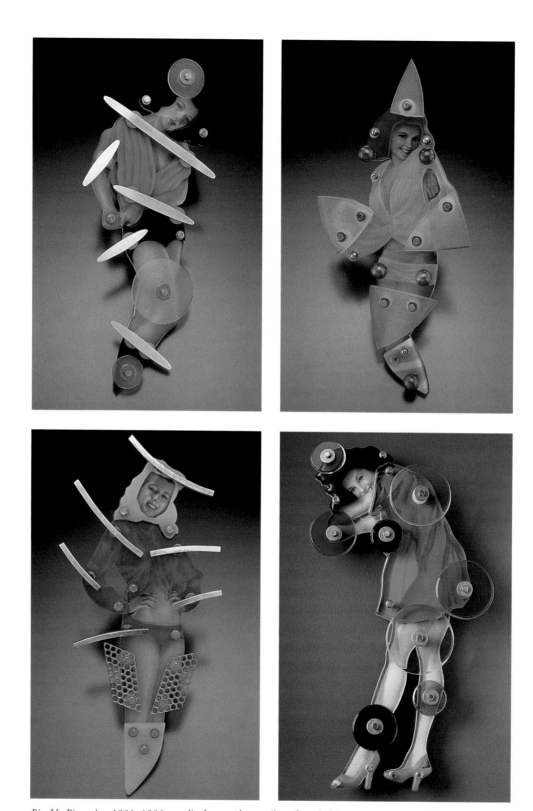

Pin-Up Pin series, 1991–1996, acrylic, bronze, brass, silver, found objects, pin-up postcards circa 1930, each approx. 2.25" x 5.5". CLOCKWISE FROM UPPER LEFT: *"Why we're barely acquainted," "Maybe I should show more discretion," "He saw right through my little scheme," "I'm single, but that could be altered."*

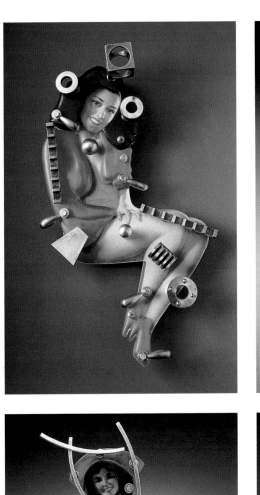

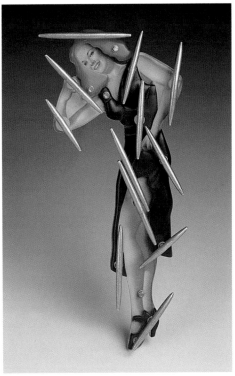

Pin-Up Pin series, 1991–1996, acrylic, bronze, brass, silver, found objects, pin-up postcards circa 1930, approx. 2.25" x 5.5". CLOCKWISE FROM UPPER LEFT: *"Do you still prefer blondes?"* (collection of Rimas Vis-Girda), *"I got a little behind in my rent," "Thumb fun, eh, kid?," "Boy, do I mow 'em down."*

"Some years ago I encountered a service that used your horoscope to determine the best place on the planet for you to live. I didn't need to employ this service to know that New Orleans was the place for me.

When I was still working in New Hampshire, an artist colleague and dear old friend, David Musson, encouraged me to consider exhibiting my work at the New Orleans Jazz & Heritage Festival. I finally agreed and was accepted to exhibit at the festival in 1977. When I arrived in New Orleans for the event I felt, in every sense of the term, that I had come home.

I know I'm not the first person or artist on whom New Orleans has had this effect, but I felt I could have been — the feeling was that profound. After that visit, I came back every year, staying longer and longer until, by the mid-1980s, I realized I was living here.

The sensory impact of New Orleans is astounding: the architecture, the food, the culture, the environment of the lake and the river and the bayous. The city is an island, and it's unique as an island city because it's surrounded by water in three different forms: the lake on the north, the river on the south, and the bayous and swamps on the east and west.

Most importantly, New Orleans is not an American city. Its only connection to the United States is its location on the North American continent. But, in fact, it's a Caribbean rim city, a northern Caribbean city; it has more to do with Havana than Atlanta. It was settled primarily by people coming not down the continent, but up from the Caribbean. With them they brought the international cuisines and languages that have become the heart and soul, the personality of the place. New Orleans is the most European city in the country. That fact struck me in my heart of hearts."

ABOVE: *Conray Fontenot,* 1992, from the *Cajun Musician Pin* series, silver, acrylic, bronze, brass, found objects, 4" x 3".
OPPOSITE: *Cajun Musician Pin* series, 1992, acrylic, bronze, brass, silver, found objects, various sizes.

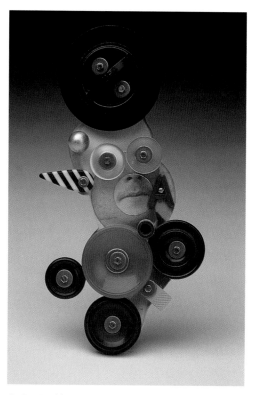

DaDa Daddy No. 1, 1996, from the *Button Pin*
series, antique photo, acrylic, brass, buttons, found
objects, 1.75" x 3".

DaDa Daddy No. 2, 1996, from the *Button Pin*
series, antique photo, acrylic, brass, buttons, found
objects, 1.75" x 3".

B Girl, 1997, from the *Button Pin* series, antique photo, acrylic, brass, buttons, found objects, 3" x 5.5".

Rabbit Girl, 1996, from the *Button Pin* series, antique photo, acrylic, brass, buttons, found objects, 3" x 5".

Oreo Cookie Dispenser Box, 1981, wood, paint, aluminum, electrical, electronic circuitry, wire, acrylic, cookies, 8" x 32" x 7". Pull the handle and a cookie slides down the chute while the counter in the hand at the top counts the take.

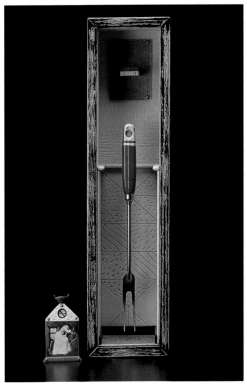

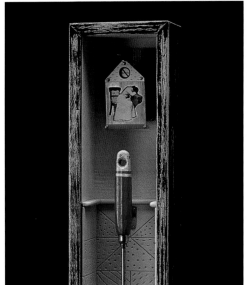

Rust Never Sleeps with *Circle Brooch,* triptych panel with removable brooch, 1990, rusted steel, acrylic, brass, aluminum, 22"H x 11"W. Collection of Abrasha Staszewski and Maria Christini.

No More Housework, 1989, sculpture box constructions with removable brooch, wood, glass, acrylic, nickel, paper, photograph, found objects, 22"H x 8"W x 5"D; brooch: 2" x 3.25". This box is a salute to the drudgery of housework. It contains a wearable, removable brooch that includes an antique photograph of a woman weeping at a table and the international NO HOUSEWORK symbol.

Cabin Fever, 1991, *Collage Box & Brooch* series, with removable, wearable brooch, wood, glass, aluminum, acrylic, nickel, brass, antique photograph, brooch: 2" x 3.5"; box: 14"H x 8"W x 5"D; backboard box: 23" x 3" x 26".

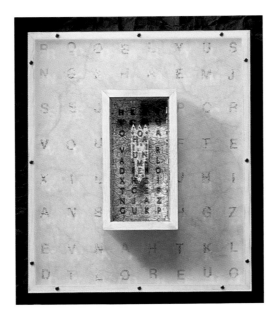

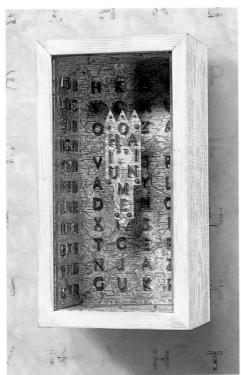

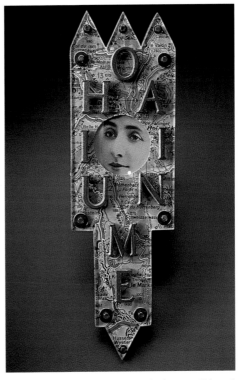

Memory Map, 1991, *Collage Box & Brooch* series, with removable, wearable brooch, wood, glass, sandblasted acrylic, paper, zinc, antique photo, brooch: 2.5" x 4"; box: 8" x 5" x 14"; backboard box: 23" x 3" x 26".

Juggler, 1991, *Collage Box & Brooch* series, with removable, wearable brooch, wood, glass, aluminum, acrylic, nickel, brass, antique photograph, electrical wiring, brooch: 2" x 3.5"; box: 8" x 5" x 14"; backboard box: 23" x 3" x 26".

Nesouaquoit, 1995, *Original Inhabitant* series, sculpture box with removable, wearable brooch, wood, birch bark, paper, copper, brass, silver, acrylic, box: 14" x 18" x 5"; brooch: 3.25"Dɪᴀ. Complete series (six pieces) part of the permanent collection of the Renwick Gallery of the Smithsonian Institution, Washington, DC.

Tokacou, 1995, *Original Inhabitant* series, sculpture box with removable, wearable brooch, wood, birch bark, paper, copper, brass, silver, acrylic, box: 14" x 18" x 5"; brooch: 2.75" x 4.5". Complete series (six pieces) part of the permanent collection of the Renwick Gallery of the Smithsonian Institution, Washington, DC.

Nowaykesugga, 1995, *Original Inhabitant* series, sculpture box with removable, wearable brooch, wood, birch bark, paper, copper, brass, silver, acrylic, box: 14" x 18" x 5"; brooch: 2.5" x 5.25". Complete series (six pieces) part of the permanent collection of the Renwick Gallery of the Smithsonian Institution, Washington, DC.

ABOVE LEFT: *Mythos Vanity,* 1996, wood, glass, paint, steel wire, galvanized steel, stones, found objects, 28" x 21" x 29". ABOVE RIGHT: View of open drawer that holds two photo-collage pins thematically connected to the vanity. BOTTOM: *Chicken Coop Studio,* Vinalhaven, ME, July 28, 1993; 5:00 a.m. View of almost completed *Mytho*s *Vanity* and the artist.

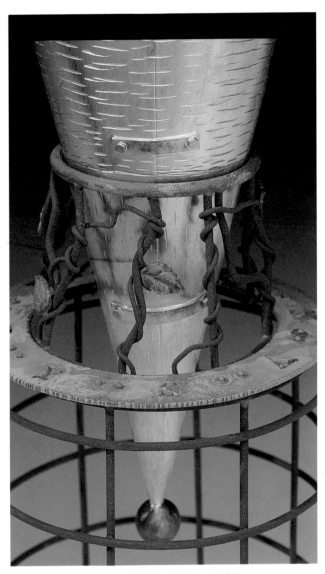

Sanctify, 1998, kiddush cup, steel, bronze, silver, 5"H x 3"DIA, cup with holder 4.5"DIA x 12"H.

TOP: *Teapot* (group), 1994, patinated brass, average size 6"DIA x 18"H. BOTTOM: Installation photo, *TWIST,* 1994, Portland, OR.

Everyday Object #18 - Telephone, 1995, steel, telephone parts, 5.5" x 8.5" x 8".

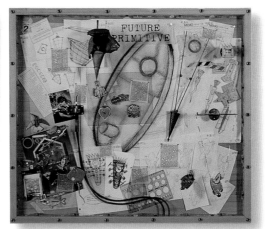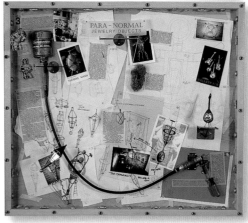

423D-think.draw.make, 1994, wood and acrylics with various other materials, each panel: 4" x 30" x 34". CLOCK-
WISE FROM TOP LEFT: *Panel No. 1: Heartwear; Panel No. 2: Future Primitive; Panel No. 3: Para-Normal; Panel 4:
Techno-Romantic.*

BEING 20 — (1967)
FIRST BUSINESS SINCE THE LEMONADE STAND

"I was in my second year of college. I was adrift. The Phys. Ed. major of the previous year
fizzled as my creative interests bubbled to the surface. Still on the gymnastics team, I was
forging my advisor's signature and taking every art, music and philosophy course I could
get into. I was making jewelry on the side as well, fraternity and sorority pins and, of
course, bangle bracelets. During the spring of 1967, a friend of mine, Fred, approached
me with the idea of opening a silversmith shop. He'd do the sales; I'd make the jewelry.
We opened the Golden Owl in East Stroudsburg, Pennsylvania, in June. I worked during

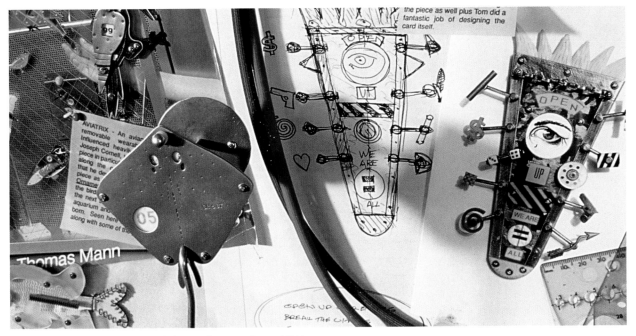

Details of panels from 423D-*think.draw.make,* a traveling exhibition.

the day in the shop and in the afternoons and evenings I worked with my theater professor, Rob Howell, in a summer stock theater called Cherry Lane. We did melodramas. I acted, helped create the sets and got around on a Honda motorcycle. It was a busy, wonderful summer, and at the end of it, Fred disappeared with a bunch of cash never to be seen again. I'd borrowed money from some friends who'd all agreed to be paid back in jewelry, which I did by November.

The following summer (1968), Jack and Jade Deignan invited me to open a silversmith shop in the rear of their Surf Shop in Stone Harbor, New Jersey. For the next five summers we ran a successful summer seaside business, Solar Wind. Eventually, it grew to three shops in Avalon, Stone Harbor and Wildwood. We had a great time doing the surf thing. In 1970, my brother Todd joined the team, and we started a partnership that would last until 1977.

During the summer of 1969, we all gave up surfing for a week and went to Woodstock. That experience changed everything. For the first time, in the forest up the hill from the stage, I saw craft artists selling their work from homemade booths. I was totally mesmerized and energized by the idea of traveling around the country to present and sell my work in the same manner."

BEING 30 — (1977)

REINVENTION/TRANSITION TIME

"Todd and I decided to continue our summer business through the fall, winter and spring. In the fall of 1971 we opened Earthlight Supply, a combination natural food store and silversmith shop in the Pocono Mountains. We did our first art fair in Winter Park, Florida, the following March, and the next spring we did the first American Craft Council show at Rhinebeck, New York. That year we bought a building and opened Mountain Gallery, with Earthlight Supply in a rented building just down the street.

During this period I began to experiment with the application of collage and assemblage techniques in jewelry making. We made our living on polished silver jewelry, but I was gradually moving away from that look as I developed a personal design aesthetic. By 1977, I'd had enough of the Solar Wind Silversmiths thing and promoted the breakup of our partnership. Todd bought me out of the natural food store and ran it himself for the next ten years. We sold the building and the gallery business, and I moved my studio to my home in the woods outside of town. For the next five years I worked studiously at developing what would become, by 1982, the Techno-Romantic design vocabulary. This was the 'starving artist' period of my career, but it was full of big fun. By 1982 I'd made the transition from doing craft as a lifestyle to making it my profession."

There Is a Rock in Each of Us, 1994, hanging *Space Frame Sculpture,* brass, steel, aluminum, stone, 12"Dɪᴀ x 26"L.

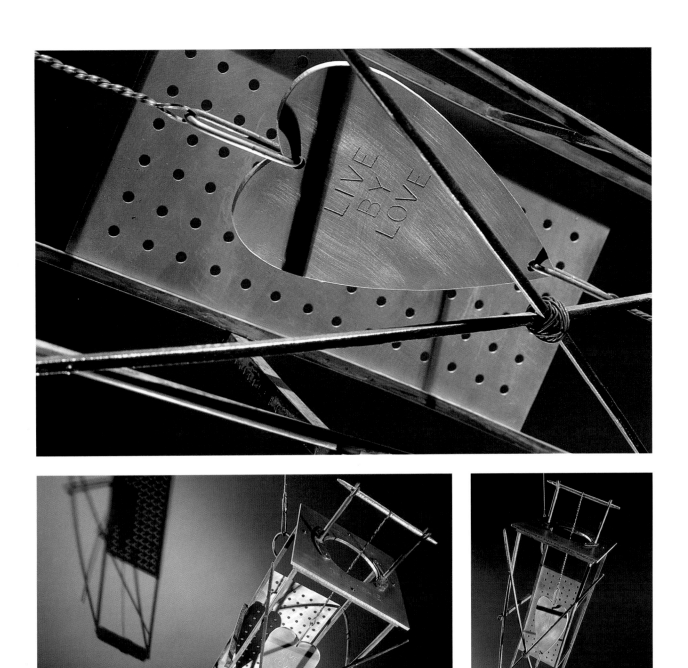

Live by Love, 1994, *Space Frame Sculpture,* brass, steel, aluminum, 12" x 12" x 30".

BEING 40 — (1987)

TAKING THE REAL WORLD PLUNGE

"I enjoyed an incredible lifestyle for much of the 1980s. I spent summer and fall in Portsmouth, New Hampshire, working in a great studio in the Button Factory, and winters and spring in New Orleans in a shotgun house that was both home and studio. I had a house in Kittery, Maine, just across the river from Portsmouth and an apartment in New Orleans in the Garden District. I had employees in both places and was able to keep it all coordinated and humming along. Then reality struck in the form of advice from my accountant. She told me I was blowing my money on lifestyle (and wasn't it sweet!) and that I should start thinking about the future. The suggestion, taken reluctantly to heart, was to invest in real estate.

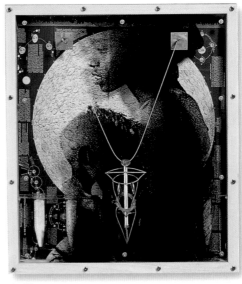

Goddess No. 1, 1993, sculpture box with *Space-Frame Neckpiece,* from *Food for Thought* traveling exhibition, wood, silver, bronze, acrylic, milk powder, paper w/screened image, 21" x 31" x 4".

In the spring of '87, I began the search for properties in earnest. Always attuned to serendipity, I noticed a 'For Sale' sign on the building next door to the studio of my photographer, Will Crocker, when I stopped in to have some work shot. Three days later I had an accepted offer on 5,000 square feet of commercial real estate. The studio was installed in the renovated building and opened for work in January of '88. The gallery opened in November of the same year.

Four years later, I acquired a second building two doors down the street and installed my private studio on the second floor. The first floor became I/O+, the museum gift store concept that actually supported the gallery's viability as a presentation space."

Food for Thought, 1993, installation view of wall treatment, Gallery I/O, New Orleans.

BEING 50 — (1997)
REINVENTION TIME AGAIN

"Philosophy: The climb to the top isn't nearly as hard as staying on top. You don't notice the effort it takes while you're building; you only notice the effort it takes when you're maintaining. It becomes clear that it's time to take all of the learning and experience acquired up to this point and apply it to the next phase of life and career. I jokingly tell colleagues that I have just graduated from the Art Institute of Hard Knocks with an MFA, an MBA, and a Doctorate in

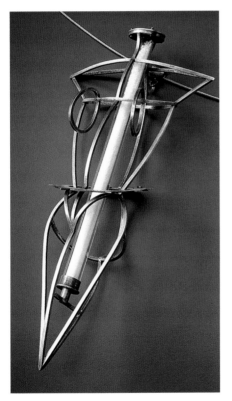

Goddess No. 1, 1993, *Space-Frame Neckpiece.*

Psychology. In some ways, it feels like I've finally embarked on a real career as an artist.

Fact: We've occupied the buildings on Magazine Street for ten years. Gallery I/O (for "insight full objects") has been enormously successful in establishing a market for contemporary jewelry and furniture design in New Orleans. The Techno-Romantic line has been climbing steadily, increasing its gross income by 30-40% a year since 1982.

But there are clouds on the horizon. The look that Thomas Mann and Techno-Romantic have established is now being widely imitated. It's become a genre, and lower-priced imitative work dilutes the market and diminishes my own sales. We're topped out in our pricing and have, to a certain extent, saturated our own market. It's time to reinvent at every level.

In January of 1997, we launched a new e-commerce website to replace the homemade version we put up in '95. We published our first retail catalog in 1998. We downsized the gallery and renamed it Thomas Mann Gallery. The business is leaner and meaner. We've refloated the boat and course-corrected for the future. The sailing looks good!

At the same time, this reinvention is taking place artistically. Since January 2000, I've been busy inventing a new design vocabulary and experimenting with the public response to it. This new direction is being sent out under the name Thomas Robert Mann. It has its roots in Techno-Romantic but is a major move away from that seminal look. Launched in February 2001, TRM (as we call it in-house) has enjoyed a quizzical but enthusiastic response."

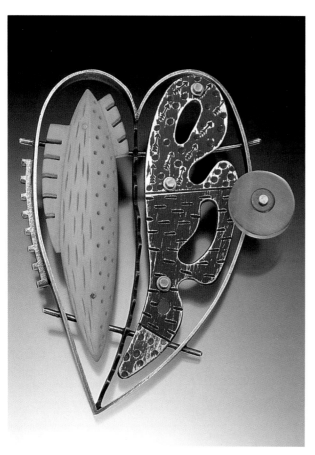

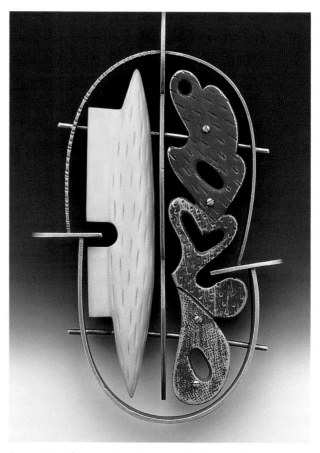

Heart, 2000, *Float* series brooch, silver, brass, aluminum, paint, micarta, 3" x 4".

Deco, 2000, *Float* series brooch, silver, aluminum, paint, micarta, 3" x 5.25".

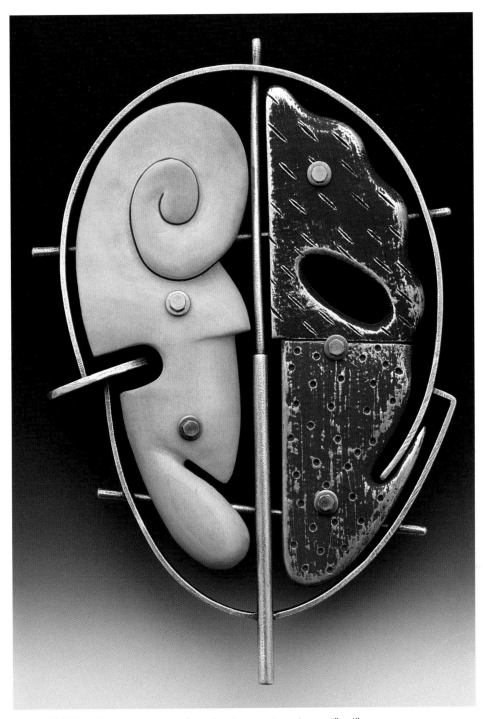

Amoeboid, 2000, *Float* series brooch, silver, aluminum, paint, micarta, 3" x 4".

"At a certain point in your career you have to assume responsibility for that career and accept roles that you may have become an artist in order to avoid. In the United States, artists don't enjoy the kind of government support that other countries offer their artists, so our survival skills have to be more acute. This means that you must do things that in a more supportive environment you might be able to avoid. One of them is becoming 'the boss.'

I've never wanted to be the boss of anything except my own career. I've always preferred to work alone. But it's inevitable that you're going to need help. You just can't do by yourself all the things that need to be done to have a successful career. And there are some tasks that should be done by people who do them better than you do. Like bookkeeping!

I contend that you should never delegate a task that you haven't first mastered yourself. You can't judge another's performance unless you know what it actually takes to do the job. But any artist who thinks this is a solo trip is bound to stall out. The critical difference is always going to be the support.

The concept of 'right livelihood' is one I picked up and absorbed during the cultural angst of the late sixties. That term means that everything is right with the work you choose to do and the way in which the work is accomplished and, most importantly, whom it is shared with. My personal take on being the boss is based on this. It's my job to make the right livelihood that I've chosen and created for myself and to share with those who feel this might be right for them. Then it's my job to float the boat and keep it on course.

Having employees is one of the most challenging tasks you'll ever assume. Dealing with someone else's perception of reality as it intersects, segues or clashes with your own, nurturing their performance while keeping the boat on course, all of this will make you grow in ways you hadn't imagined. I feel like a dad a lot of the time, having to correct and correct and direct until they get it without the assistance. Then they quit and move on and you hope you part as friends and that they use the knowledge and skills they gained and come back someday to thank you for the experience. Whew!"

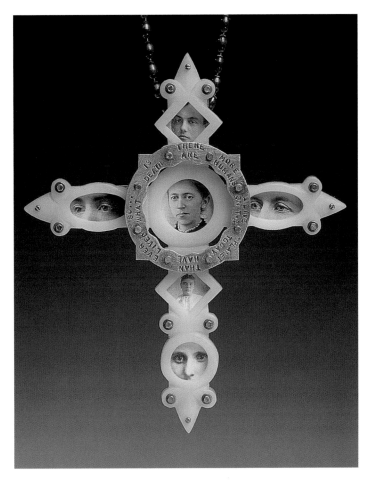

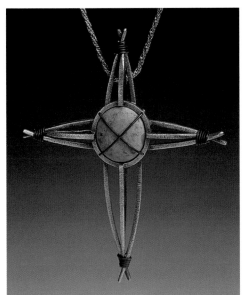

TOP: *Souls Cross,* 1997, *Cross* series, carved glow-in-the-dark acrylic, silver, antique photographs, 3" x 4.5".
LEFT: *Stone Fetish Cross,* 1997, *Cross* series, silver, iron wire, beach pebble, 2.5" x 3.75". RIGHT: *Collage Cross,*
1997, *Cross* series, photo-etched brass, laminated acrylic, bronze, silver, 2.25" x 3.25".

Swingle Earrings, 1988, bronze, brass, nickel, laminated acrylic, 1.25" x 2.25". Collection of Barbara Mueller.

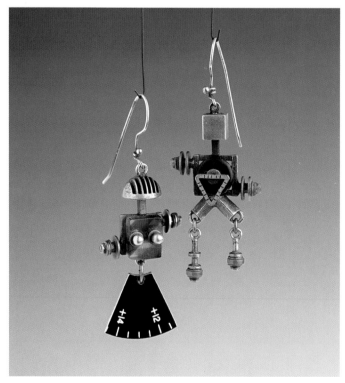

Robot Earrings, 1987, bronze, brass, nickel, laminated acrylic, 1.25" x 2.25". Collection of Mary Ellen Langsdorf.

Icon Series Pin, 1986, bronze, brass, nickel, laminated acrylic, 2.75" x 3". Collection of Judith Winig.

"When I first taught the "Design *for* Survival" workshop at Penland School in 1989, I didn't know how much impact it would have. I know now that the need for this kind of information runs deep. Recently, a student who had taken the workshop in Seattle just three years ago told me that what she learned that weekend gave her all the tools she needed to become the successful metal artist she is today.

I formulated the first version of the course as a personal challenge. I wanted to see if all of the things I'd learned in 20 years as a professional craft artist could be of value to other artists. As I began this 'mission,' I remembered the childhood story of Johnny Appleseed. He traveled the country sowing seeds, promoting the popularity of fruit tree husbandry. He wanted there to be apple trees everywhere. Like Mr. Appleseed, I wanted to plant seeds that would grow successful artists.

To challenge artists to wed their creative and technical talents to their nascent entrepreneurial abilities, I designed a rigorous two-week 'designers boot camp.' Participants were given the task of designing and fabricating one-of-a-kind work; deciphering a design vocabulary from this work; and inventing a production line based on an abbreviated family of design components from that vocabulary. Parallel to this effort, the artists learned computer skills for writing about the work; producing artist statements and press releases; designing and producing collateral business materials, stationery systems, catalog sheets and mailers. Participants also learned spreadsheet programs in order to construct cost analyses and pricing models. At the conclusion of the course, they presented their completed 'line,' their business graphics package and their press kits to a panel of buyers brought in to critique their efforts.

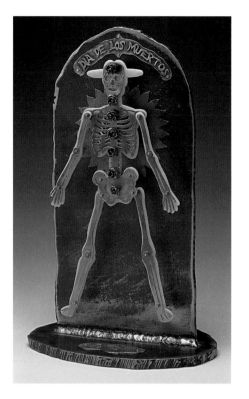

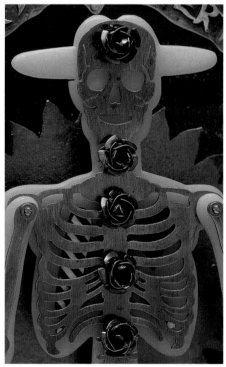

Day of the Dead sculpture with removable pin, 1997, steel, brass, nickel, glow-in-the-dark acrylic, 6" x 14", brooch (detail shown): 4" x 9".

Day of the Dead brooch, 1998, silver, glow-in-the-dark acrylic, laminated acrylic, 3.25" x 5.5".

As word got out about this unusual course, I began to receive requests to teach it in other places. When the original two-week scenario couldn't be accommodated, I had to condense the course into a two-day event. In the process I had to focus on the essential components of my message: design vocabulary, public relations and pricing.

I want to help shift the paradigm of how artists go about the work of existing in our culture. I look forward to a time when being an artist is seen not as a difficult, unrewarding career path, but as one which is encouraged, supported and rewarded. I want to live in a world where parents encourage their children to follow their artistic dreams because they know everyone wants art and will buy it! The "Design *for* Survival" workshops and lectures are my humble attempt to affect this shift.

It's a big dream but not an impossible one."

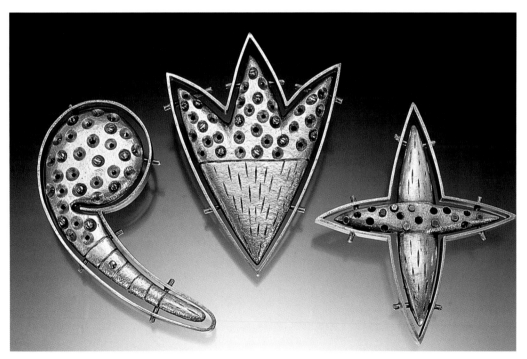

Float series brooches (group), 2000, silver, aluminum, various sizes.

OPPOSITE: *Book Locket,* 1996, silver, brass, 1.5"H x 1"W x .25"D.

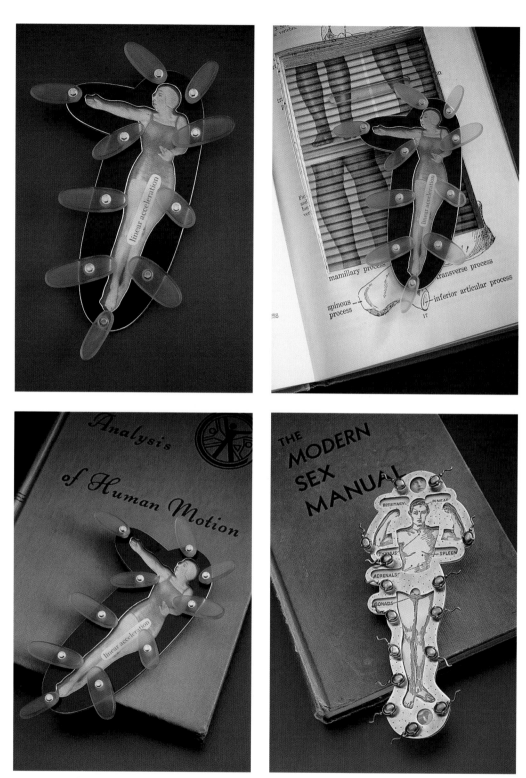

Book Pin series with removable, wearable brooches, paper, acrylic, anodized aluminum, brass, book illustrations, found objects. ABOVE AND BOTTOM LEFT: *Analysis of Human Motion,* 1994, brooch, 2.5" x 4". BOTTOM RIGHT: *The Modern Sex Manual,* 1991, brooch, 2.5" x 5.5". OPPOSITE: *Book Pin* series collection, 1991.

Chronology

1947 Thomas Robert Mann born in Northampton, Pennsylvania.

1955 Charlotte Mann enrolls her son Tom in Saturday morning art classes at the Baum Art School, Allentown, Pennsylvania. Mr. Baum explains that Tom should not come to class in the good clothes Charlotte insisted he wear, since he will mess them up within the hour; the bow tie, Baum notes, is equally useless. Tom learns to paint, sort of. More important, he learns to like to draw. This, he says, has made all the difference.

1963 Takes first jewelry course (two semesters) through high school art program.

1964-67 Works part-time in silversmith shops of C. Leslie Smith and Cinruss Creations.

1965 Begins college at East Stroudsburg University as a Physical Education major. Conflict: is the true path athletic or artistic?

1967 Opens silversmith shop, The Golden Owl, for the summer in East Stroudsburg, Pennsylvania. Designs and builds sets and acts in summer stock theater, the Cherry Lane Opera House.

1968 Opens summer silversmith shop in the rear of the Island Surf Shop in Stone Harbor, New Jersey, with partners Jade and Jack Deignan and Bill Taylor.

1969 Opens independent silversmith shop, Solar Wind, with partners, in Stone Harbor, New Jersey. Attends Woodstock music festival.

1970 Graduates with BA in Performing Arts. Continues summer businesses. Brother Todd Mann joins the Solar Wind crew in Stone Harbor.

1971 Opens Earthlight Supply in the Pocono Mountains in partnership with brother, Todd. Moves into the Dyer house on Fawn Road, where he lives for the next 12 years. Agnes Dyer was a painter in the abstract modernist mode; Tom is influenced by her style and her studio home environment.

1972 Exhibits work at first fair: Winter Park Arts Festival, Winter Park, Florida.

1973 Purchases first building and opens Mountain Gallery, with studio in rear. Tom and Todd now own three businesses in East Stroudsburg: Mountain Gallery, Solar Wind Silversmiths and Earthlight Supply (home of the Earthburger). Exhibits at American Craft Council Show at Rhinebeck, New York.

A Girl and Her Fish, 1989, photo-collage pin, brass, bronze, sandblasted acrylic, antique French postcard, 2.5" x 3.25".

1977 Businesses dissolved. Todd continues Earthlight Supply; Tom explores new creative territory. Exhibits for first time at New Orleans Jazz & Heritage Festival. Returns to New Orleans for longer periods each year; by 1982 has established a home and studio there.

1980 Exhibits new body of work, entitled Heartware (later Techno-Romantic), at the Lakefront Festival of Arts, Milwaukee, Wisconsin.

1982 Inspired by the long-held desire to be a Sea Scout, moves to Portsmouth, New Hampshire, to be near the ocean. Acquires a sailboat and a studio in the Button Factory artist loft building. Lives and works, seasonally, in Portsmouth and New Orleans for the next five years.

A Boy and His Dog, 1989, photo-collage pin, brass, bronze, sandblasted acrylic, laminated acrylic, antique French postcard, 2" x 3.25".

1985 Travels to Europe. Attends American Craft Council exchange show in Paris and the Salone del Mobile in Milan. Visits Aix-en-Provence, St.-Paul-de-Vence, Florence, Venice and Cinque Terre.

1987-88 Buys and renovates building at 1810 Magazine Street in New Orleans; opens Thomas Mann Design in January 1988 and Gallery I/O in November 1988.

1989 Travels to Japan; exhibits and lectures in Nagoya and Kyoto. Teaches the "Design for Survival" course for the first time at Penland School, Penland, North Carolina.

1990 Travels to Mexico; visits Mexico City, Teotihuacan and Michoacan.

1993 Acquires second property at 1804 Magazine Street. Opens I/O+.

1995 Travels to France and England. Launches the *OXIDATION/BURIAL* project while summering on Vinalhaven.

1997 Travels to Hawaii and Australia for exhibitions and lectures in Honolulu, Sydney and Brisbane.

2000 Begins retrieval of the *OXIDATION/BURIAL* project.

2001 Graduates from School of Hard Knocks with MFA, MBA. Begins second phase of career.

A c k n o w l e d g m e n t s

No artist can be successful without support. Success is always attributable to a complex web of nurturing influence, inspiration, patronage and assistance. Here is mine.

Partners, Patrons, Colleagues, Friends & Family • Florence Baldwin • Shan Bauer • Charlie & Peg Bishop • Chud & Babs Bensinger • Xavier & Ellie Blaschka • Peter Carlson • Pierre Cavalan • Kenny Charbonnet • Tom Cowgill • Will Crocker • Jade & John Deignan • Tom Diel • Steve Elling • Rick Fifield • John Flemming • Mark Garcie • Ani & Gil Helmick • Rob & Joan Howell • Phil & Sandy Jurus • Jim Kunkel • Kenn Kushner • Susan Lange • Bernice & Ed Levin • Terri Logan • Keiko & Michael Magyar • Charlotte & Robert Mann • Todd, Zachary & Cathy Mann • Lee Angelo Marracini • John Martini • Helma Mezey • Mike McHugh • Elsie Michie • Bob & Eileen Miner • Steve Morrell • Gabriel Ofiesh • Tom Paquin • Paige Rogers • Penny & David Ross • John Rummler • Biba Schutz • Sam Shaw • Sterling Strauser • Nancy, Nathan & John Slonaker • Rob & Pam Steeg • Bill Taylor • Francois Tresfort • Doc Wolfe

Thomas Mann Design staff, 1992

Coworkers 1968 to 2001 • *Stone Harbor* • Peter Carlson • Phil Lange • Chuck Stump • *East Stroudsburg* • Mitzi Bensinger • Susan Bradford • Eric Cartwright • Brent Cartwright • Julia Clauss • Bob Davies • Jill Elizabeth • Tom Eshelman • Donna Ferret • Penny Hamilton-Ely • Gail Howard • Wendy Mettler • Ruth Sypian • Gary Werkheiser • *Portsmouth* • Rita Benesch • Carolyn Burgess • Brian Busta • Jenny Chichester • Dierdre Donchian • Carol Kelly • Angela Papoutsy • Lisa Poore • Meagan Stelzer • Willow Stelzer • Julie White • Chris Williams • *New Orleans* • Samara Aldern • Katie Allen • Bridget Bailey • Cynthia Barber • Brent Barnidge • Fabienne Barrau • Frank Basile • JoAnn Blohowiak • Lori Boornazian • Suzanne Bottoms • Matthew Boutte • Keena Bradford • Sam Brantley • Hopi Breton • Stephanie Bruno • Robin Buckalew • Allison Buchsbaum • Lance Campbell • Ryan Caplinger • Selene Carter • Jim Charbonnet • Yvonne Cheoun • Audra Choate • Peggy Cochran • Ralph Cole • Ricardo Constanza • Cathy Cooper • Colin Cowan • Tom Cowgil • Lucas Cox • Lisa Cressionie • Ben Curtis • Jane Decuers • Pilar DeLeon • Jeannie Detweiler • Jennifer Dewey • Tom Diel • Jacqueline Dinwiddie • Russ Dozier • Michele DuBos • Karen Eblen • Catherine Ellender • Greg Enslen • Elizabeth Fahey • Shane Fell • Heather Ferrell • Mot Filipowski • Noel Fisher • Casey Frankenberger • Mark Garcie • Eden Gass • Alden Genre • Kim Glosserman • Lisa Glosserman • Devra

1995

Goldstein • Tiffany Goodall • Laura Goulas • Robert Grimes • Brent Guarisco • Paul Guerra • Jill Halpern • Marilee Hanemann • Travis Hanson • Heidi Hayne • Eric Healan • Lizzy Hermann • Cassandra Jackson • Alison James • Tracey Johnson • Shanti Johnson • Tina Johnson • Tracy Kennan • Michelle Kline • Julie Koebbe • Mary Kosut • Katie Kyle • Mary Landy • Misti Larkin • Lisa Lazano • Lorna Leedy • Rod Lemaire • Jeffrey Leon • Monique Leon • Rubin Lindsey • Marz Livingston • Robyn Loda • Daphne Loney • Joe Lowe • William Lowe • Ingrid MacWatt • Sara Mann • Marcus Marino • Wendy Martin • Shannon Mathis • Halimah McClelland • Gene Menerey • Helma Mezey • Courtney Miller • Dave Miss • Michelle Mock • Kate Montgomery • Page Moran • Steve Morrell • David Morrow • Marcie Moss • Sheinita Moten • Ian Mount • Amy Moyers • Richard Mueller • Richard Mueller • Page Nall • James Naquin • Jean Marie Nestor • Charlotte Nolan Byrd • Beth Normile • Koki Otero • Thomas Paquin • Drew Pelias • Maria Pham • Poppy Platzek • Suzanne Powney • Heather Preist • Kristin Prol • Carrie Quandt • Amy Rainero • Colleen Ramagoz • Caroline Rankin • Sunday Richardson • Laura Richens • Rebecca Rigney • Babette Rittenberg • Paige Rogers • Stella Rogers • Russ Ross • Dashka Roth

• Locksley Rushworth • Monica Sanusi Gelé • Tim Schmid • Michael Selle • Peter Senesac • Elizabeth Shannon • Patricia Sills • Natalie Simmons • Vanessa Skantze • Ruth Sladovich • Patty Smith • Patricia Smith • Sarah Soffer • Kristin Speier • Kim Spranley • James Stanton • Ken Strausbaugh • Katie Taylor • Melissa Thompson • Caroline Trespel • Elizabeth Underwood • Jennifer Underwood • Matthew VanBesien • Michael Robert Vaughn • Nguy Vu • Tanya Waller • Roberta Williams • Cindy Williams • Margaret Williams • Sam Winchester • Patrick Wood • Khadem Zaved • My apologies to anyone I may have missed

Professional Support • Ruth & Rick Snyderman, Works Gallery, Philadelphia, PA • Libby & JoAnn Cooper, Mobilia Gallery, Cambridge, MA • Pam Glosserman & Eve France, Eve France Gallery, Houston, TX • Lisa & Kim Glosserman, High Gloss, Houston, TX • Mary Hammatt • Lauren & Paul Schneider, Twist, Portland, OR • Richard & Suzanne Langman, Langman Gallery, Willow Grove, PA • Bob Libby, Spectrum Galleries, Brewster, MA • Eureka Crafts, Syracuse, NY • Nancy & Alan Saturn, American Artisan Gallery, Nashville, TN • Susan Cummins, Susan Cummins Gallery, Mill Valley, CA • Linda Given, Joie de Vivre, Cambridge, MA • Priscilla van Loon, Gallery 33, Portsmouth, NH • Elouise Evans Rusk, Obsidian Gallery, Tucson, AZ • John Martini, Lucky Street Gallery, Key West, FL • Sal Scaglione & Dana Heacock, Abacus, Portland, ME • Marcia Smith, Gallery Ten, New York, NY • Mark Milliken, Mark Milliken Gallery, New York, NY • Barbara & Robert Kaylor, R. Grey Gallery, Boise, ID • Lynn Allinger & Gary Stamm, Craft Co. No. 6, Rochester, NY • Paula & Henry Leighton, Beautiful Things Gallery, Scotch Plains, NJ • Sandra Ainsley, Sandra Ainsley Gallery, Toronto, Canada • American Craft Council • Arts Council of New Orleans • Nancy Sachs, Nancy Sachs Gallery, St. Louis, MO • Erica Netsky, Netsky Gallery, Miami, FL • Mia, Mia Gallery, Seattle, WA • Penland School of Crafts, Penland, NC • Peters Valley Craft School, Layton, NJ • Arthur & Leah Grohe, Signature Gallery, Boston, MA • Ward Wallau • Louisiana Division of the Arts • Southern Arts Federation • National Endowment for the Arts • Contemporary Arts Center, New Orleans, LA • Toni Sikes • Roseann Raab

1999

2001

Influence & Inspiration • Laurie Anderson • Piers Anthony • Sri Aurobindo • Harry Bertoia • The Beatles • The Bible • E. Power Biggs • Tom Blair • Madame Blavatsky • Constantin Brancusi • Stewart Brand • J. Brennan • Claus Bury • David Byrne • John Cage • Alexander Calder • George Carlin • Carlos Castaneda • Anton Cepka • Arthur C. Clark • Joseph Cornell • George Corson • R. Crumb • e.e. cummings • Ram Dass • Margaret DePatta • Bob Dylan • Marcel Duchamp • Bob Ebendorf • Paul Ehrlich • Black Elk • Brian Eno • Max Ernst • Fabulous Furry Freak Brothers • Lawrence Ferlingetti • Chaz Filanowicz • Robert Frost • Buckminster Fuller • Mahatma Gandhi • Allen Ginsburg • Phillip Glass • Bill Graham • Martha Graham • Eileen Gray • Dick Gregory • G.I. Gurdjieff • Rich Harper • Jimi Hendrix • Frank Herbert • Steve Hoag • Abbie Hoffman • Rob Howell • Aldus Huxley • Janis Joplin • Herman Junger • Hazrat Inayat Khan • Sam Kramer • Jim Kweskin • Ursula LaGuin • Timothy Leary • Annie Lennox • Ed Levin • John Lily • René Magritte • Herman Melville • Eleanor Moty • Jim Musselman • David Musson • Friedrich Nietzsche • Louise Nevelson • P.D. Ouspensky • Earl Pardon • Robert Persig • Pablo Picasso • Bob Place • Jacques Prévert • Wendy Ramshaw • Man Ray • Lou Reed • Vernon Reed • Wilhelm Reich • Eleanor Roosevelt • Erik Satie • Oskar Schlemmer • Kiff Slemmons • C. Leslie Smith • Patti Smith • Constantin Stanislavski • Philippe Starck • Rudolph Steiner • Sterling Strauser • Talking Heads • Vladimir Tatlin • Paul Tillich • Pir Vilyat • Andy Warhol • Alan Watts • Wim Wenders • J. Fred Woell • John Yo • Paramhansa Yoganada • Tadanori Yokoo • Frank Zappa • Baum School of Art • Firesign Theatre • Jiddu Krishnamurti • Vinalhaven, ME • Immanuel Velikovsky

FOR BOB

Industry statistics indicate that 98% of all people who ever have knowledge of an artist's work will do so through the printed image. That fact makes good photography essential to an artist's success. I want to thank all of the photographers whose work appears on these pages for their honest and good work. I especially wish to thank Will Crocker, who has been making my work look great since the early 1980s. His creative brilliance is responsible for making this book the visual gem I believe it is.

Photographer Credits
Wendy Andriga: 105 • Bob Barrett: 25, 43 top, 69 top left, 70 top • Paula Burch: 19 • Will Crocker: jacket (front and back), frontispiece, copyright page, 6, 11, 12, 13, 15, 16 bottom, 28 top, 31 top, 42, 43 bottom, 44 bottom, 46, 47, 48, 50, 52, 53, 61, 68 top left/bottom right, 74 all, 75, 76, 77, 78, 79 all, 81, 82 top right, 83, 84 all, 85, 86, 88 all, 89 all, 90, 91, 93 left, 94, 95 all, 96 all, 97 all, 98 all, 99 both, 100 both, 101 both, 106 all, 110 top, 111, 121, 122, 123 • Strode Ekert: 108 both, 109 all • Sarah Essex: 10, 54 all, 56, 58 bottom, 59, 62, 63, 65, 66 all, 69 bottom right, 116 both, 117 • Ralph Gabriner: 16 top, 28 center, 68 top right/bottom left, 69 top right/bottom left, 73 all, 82 left/bottom right, 92 both, 93 right, 120, 124, 125 • Rob Karosis: 34 top/bottom • Bill Keough: 38 top/bottom right • Thomas Mann: 17 bottom, 21, 22 top, 23 center and bottom, 26, 27 bottom, 32 top left/right, 67 all, 70 bottom, 102 top right/bottom left and right, 104 bottom • Todd Mann: 23 top • Owen Murphy: 8 • Gerrod Perrone: 7, 20, 28 bottom, 31 bottom left/right, 35 bottom, 37 all, 38 top/bottom left, 57, 58 top left, 87 top left/bottom left, 103 all, 104 top, 115 all, 118 both, 119 • George Post: 17 top, 112 both, 113 • David Richmonds: 24 • Nijme Rinaldi: 29 • Bill Seitz: 102 top left • Melissa Thompson: 51

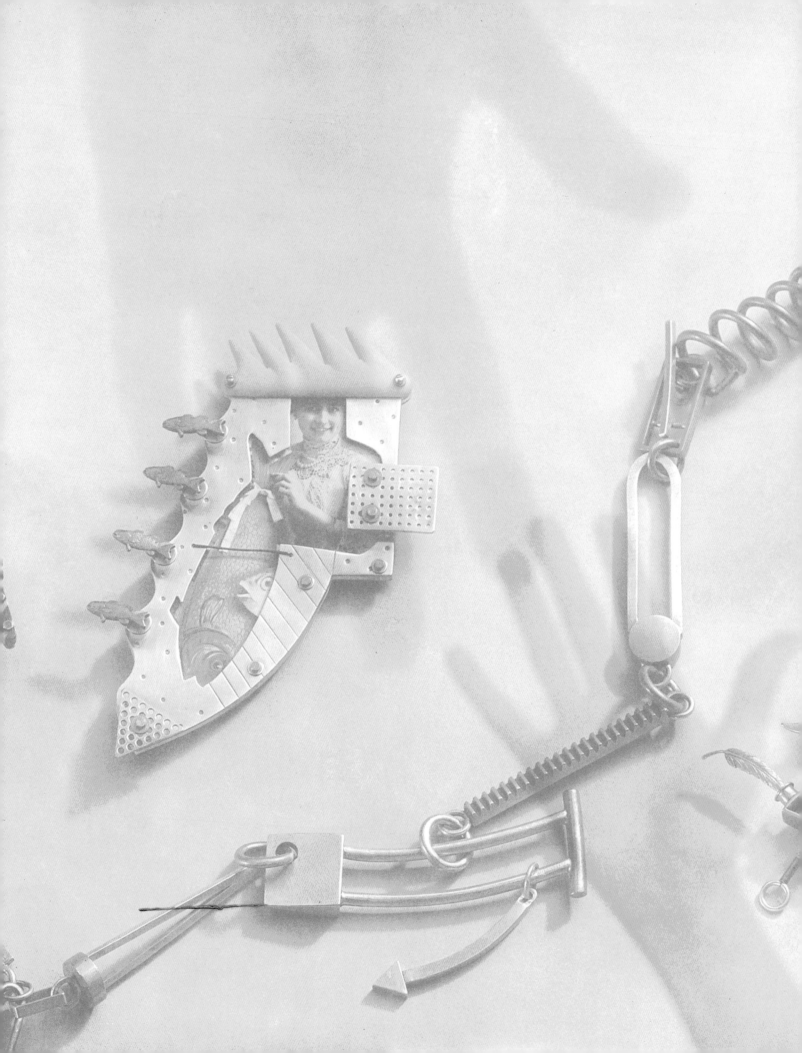